BE OUR
GUEST

REVISED AND UPDATED EDITION

BE OUR GUEST

Perfecting the Art of Customer Service

by

with Theodore Kinni

Foreword by Tom Staggs

Los Angeles   New York

For information address Disney Editions,
1101 Flower Street, Glendale, California 91201.

Printed in the United States of America
Reinforced binding

First Edition
10

FAC-020093-19168

Library of Congress Cataloging-in-Publication Data
Be our guest: perfecting the art of customer service / by Disney Institute
with Theodore Kinni; foreword by Robert A. Iger.
p. cm.
Includes bibliographical references and index.
ISBN 978-1-4231-4584-4 (alk. paper)
1. Walt Disney World (Fla.) 2. Amusement parks—Customer services—
Florida—Orlando. 3. Disney Institute. I. Kinni, Theodore B., 1956–
II. Disney Institute.
GV1853.3.F62W3417 2011
791.06875924—dc23
2011023545

The Official Disney Fan Club
D23.com

THIS LABEL APPLIES TO TEXT STOCK

Always remember, the magic begins with *you*.

Table of Contents

Foreword

BY TOM STAGGS

Like most cast members, I love hearing from my friends and family after they take a Disney vacation. As the chairman of Walt Disney Parks and Resorts, I want to know everything about their trip—where they stayed, the shows they saw, the attractions they rode, the restaurants they visited, and the food they ate. But more than anything, I want to hear exactly how our cast members made them *feel* throughout their visit.

While we may be known for our castles, mountains, cruise ships, and hotels, I believe that one of the things that most sets Disney apart is our cast—and it's their special, individualized, and unscripted interactions with guests that create the most memorable Disney moments.

Big or small, those interactions are often captured in the letters we receive from our guests every day. In fact, reading those letters is one of the most enjoyable parts of my job. They don't always mention their favorite attraction, show, or meal, but they *almost* always tell us about a cast member who made their experience unforgettable.

This is true for guests I run into in the parks as well. They love telling me all about the cast members who have made a difference in their visit. But they also seem to have one inevitable question for me.

"How does Disney do it?"

Of course, my first answer is always, "It's magic." This gets mixed reactions. Some accept this answer with a smile and give me a look that says, "I knew you were going to say that."

Others, however, press harder for concrete answers, as they genuinely want to know the secrets to how we create that magic. Some of them have businesses of their own, with a workforce to motivate, customers they need to please, and products they want to be valuable and relevant.

They want to know *exactly*, step by step, what we do to make each person feel special throughout a Disney vacation. They want to know why our cast members are always smiling—how they maintain the enthusiasm, creativity, and ability to transport guests to a place of fantasy and adventure while simultaneously making them feel right at home.

Most are quite shocked when I tell them that it isn't a secret at all. In fact, we publish a book—this book—describing precisely how we create and deliver a world-class guest experience.

And as you read through *Be Our Guest*, you'll see that our magic is both an art and a science. We start with a great story and design ideas to create an experience. We implement training and processes like any well-run company to make sure that we operate safely and efficiently. And we rely on the intuitive hospitality and friendliness of our outstanding cast to make each guest feel like we have designed the place just for them. As a result, after several decades of practice, we have combined this art and this science to build a culture of world-famous storytelling and legendary guest service.

Creating the best possible experience for our guests to share with family, friends, loved ones, and colleagues is the essence of what we do, and it defines who we are.

Individual stories, attractions, and experiences may change over time, but the expectation to deliver a magical guest experience is timeless. It is our dream and our mission to keep that magic alive, to exceed those expectations, and to welcome people around the world to be our guests for years to come.

Sincerely,

Tom Staggs
Chairman
Walt Disney Parks and Resorts

Introduction

*In this volatile business of ours, we can ill afford
to rest on our laurels, even to pause in retrospect.
Times and conditions change so rapidly that we must
keep our aim constantly focused on the future.*
—Walt Disney

Walt Disney harnessed the talents of his cast members (Disney-speak for employees) and inspired their hearts with his vision to create unparalleled entertainment experiences. He understood innately that the long-term success of his company depended upon his ability to motivate people, one day and one innovation at a time.

The year 2011 not only commemorates the 110th anniversary of Walt's birth, it also marks another important anniversary for The Walt Disney Company: the 25th year of providing "The Disney Approach" professional development programs to organizations worldwide. Tens of thousands of business practitioners in virtually every industry and country have experienced Disney Institute over the past quarter century. They have found that Disney Institute programs do much more than provide a substantial learning opportunity. These programs inspire participants to see themselves, their organizations, and the world at large in an entirely new light—using Disney best practices as their beacon.

From our earliest days, education has been a hallmark of our company. It was Walt himself who said, "We have always tried to be guided by the basic idea that, in the discovery of knowledge, there is great entertainment—as, conversely, in all good entertainment, there is always some grain of wisdom, humanity, or enlightenment to be gained." This philosophy is deeply embedded in all Disney Institute programming.

When Tom Peters and Bob Waterman profiled The Walt Disney Company (then Walt Disney Productions) in their groundbreaking 1984 book and companion video, *In Search of Excellence*, corporate eyes turned to Disney as a company that sets the benchmark for best business practices. To facilitate the benchmarking process, the Walt Disney World Resort in 1986 created a program called "The Disney Approach to People Management."

But the corporate thirst for information about the critical success factors that drive Disney's growth could not be quenched by one topic. So over the years, new programs were created around Disney's overall approach to business excellence, including creativity, leadership, customer service, and brand loyalty. In 1996, these professional development programs became the core of Disney Institute, and remain so today.

Since then, Disney Institute has worked with companies around the world, including many Fortune 500 companies, government agencies, and philanthropic, educational, and health-care institutions. We have established a significant presence in the training world based on our abilities to appeal to leaders in a broad range of organizations and to customize our content into programs that uniquely connect participants to their own heritage, values, people, and guests.

While workplace trends come and go, businesses will always need to find new and creative ways to mobilize the brainpower, passion, and creative energies of their workforce. And that's what Disney Institute is all about.

In this book, the updated 10th anniversary edition of *Be Our Guest*, we take you behind the scenes to discover Disney best practices and philosophies in action. We provide you with an insider's glimpse of the Quality Service principles in action both at The Walt Disney Company, as told from the perspectives and experiences of cast members from around the world, and in other organizations, as told by executives who have participated in Disney Institute programs.

Walt's fundamentals for success still ring true. You build the best product you can. You give people effective training to support the delivery of exceptional service. You learn from your experiences. And you celebrate success. You never stop growing. You never stop believing.

We hope this book will spark new levels of performance, productivity, and pride inside your organization by sharing some of what has made our company a legendary success over the years. But this book is only a snapshot of how we make magic every day at The Walt Disney Company. We welcome you to experience our programs for yourself.

We thank our editor, Wendy Lefkon of Disney Editions, for being the guiding force in making this project a reality. We thank Ted Kinni for crafting our story. We thank our clients for sharing their stories with our readers. Most of all, we thank the many thousands of Walt Disney cast members for their continual efforts to make a difference with guests and with each other every day.

CHAPTER 1

Disney's Approach to Quality Service

Kelvin Bailey was beginning to suspect that his boss might not be playing with a full deck. "We drove ten or twenty miles and we got into this nasty, wasted country," he recalls. "Water, swamps, jungle, alligators. I thought, 'He's got to be out of his mind—this is nothing! Water up to our knees!' You couldn't have given me the land."

It was the mid-1960s, and Kelvin, corporate pilot for Walt Disney Productions, was standing with Walt Disney in the Central Florida wilderness, just southwest of Orlando. Walt was in the process of buying 30,000 acres, or 47 square miles, that would come to be known as the Walt Disney World Resort. Even though he would not live to see the park developed, Walt had no trouble imagining it amid the Florida scrub. He pointed out Main Street, U.S.A., Fantasyland, and other nonexistent features to the thoroughly astounded pilot.[1] But even a master of creativity like Walt probably never imagined the full extent of what has become the world's number-one theme park complex or, for that matter, the growth of the company that he liked to remind people "was all started by a mouse."

To be sure, Walt was capable of big dreams. Under his direction, the Disney Studios had become the world leader in the field of animated films. The first theme park, Disneyland, was the embodiment of Walt's personal vision, and it was Walt who made the Disney brand synonymous with the finest in family entertainment. But even those accomplishments were simply a foundation for the company's eventual success. Walt's mouse would roar.

"No name shines more brightly in family entertainment than Disney," wrote Chairman and CEO Robert Iger in his annual letter to shareholders in January 2011.[2] A snapshot of Disney at the dawn of the new fiscal year revealed the world's largest media company, with five major businesses: media networks, parks and resorts, studio entertainment, consumer products, and interactive media.

The media network business is anchored by the ABC Television Network, which reaches 99 percent of all U.S. households and owns ten stations, six of which are located in the nation's top ten markets. It includes cable networks, such as ESPN, Disney Channel, SOAPnet, and an ownership stake in A&E and Lifetime, and also the thirty-seven-station Disney Radio Network. The parks and resorts business operates eleven theme parks at five resorts in the U.S., Europe, and Asia as well as the Disney Vacation Club, Disney Cruise Line, and Adventures by Disney, which conducts guided vacation tours. The studio entertainment business includes feature films, home entertainment, television distribution, the Disney Music Group, and Disney Theatrical Productions. The consumer business includes merchandise licensing, publishing, and the Disney Store retail chain, with more than 350 stores. The interactive media business, the newest in the company, is extending the Disney brand into games and online services.

Disney's businesses generated more than $38 billion in annual revenue and $7.6 billion in operating income in 2010. Walt and Roy Disney would surely have been astonished by these figures and the growth of their company. In 1966, the year Walt died, the company's entire profit was less than $12 million. That same year, Walt and Roy briefly considered merging the company with General Electric or Westinghouse in order to raise the estimated $100 million in capital needed to build Walt Disney World. Today, Disney's ever-growing parks and resort business produces more than $10 billion in annual revenue in its own right. In 2009, Disney theme parks occupied the first eight of the top ten slots in the industry. Thanks to the insight and vision of its founder and visionary, the Walt Disney World Resort is the largest of them all.

Since it opened, on October 1, 1971, Walt Disney World has expanded to encompass four theme parks, two water parks, thirty-four hotels (including those owned by other companies) with approximately 28,000 rooms, and over two hundred restaurants and eateries. It includes Downtown Disney—an entertainment and shopping district—and a dedicated wedding pavilion at the Grand Floridian Resort & Spa near the Magic Kingdom (more than a thousand couples tie the knot at Walt Disney World each year).

This is a good-size city located in an area about twice the size of Manhattan. Walt Disney World operates every day of the week, year round, and is the largest single-site employer in the U.S. It is run by a workforce of more than 62,000 cast members—that's Disney-speak for employees. The cast entertains and otherwise serves millions of guests (that's right, Disney-speak for customers) every year. This city can have hundreds of thousands of people in it on a crowded day. (To get an idea of the scale, consider that there are a half dozen physicians working at Walt Disney World who are dedicated solely to the guests.) The energy that powers this city? *Magic.*

PRACTICAL MAGIC

Magic is not a word that is much used in the corporate world. It is not listed on the standard balance sheet (although you could say that accounting intangibles such as goodwill include magic). Your accounting staff is probably not measuring magic's return on investment nor is it amortizing magic over thirty years. Magic is, however, a common word in the executive suites at The Walt Disney Company.

"Our guests want to be amazed, delighted, and entertained," says Bob Iger. "They are looking for the kind of magic that will transport them from their everyday lives into worlds that can only be created by Disney."

This is not a new theme. Bob's predecessor, Michael Eisner, also liked to talk about magic. "The magic of a Disney vacation," he said, "is to me the magic of quality, the magic of innovation, the magic of beauty, the magic of families coming together, the magic of our cast members. All of these things kind of bundle together."[3]

Just because you cannot assign a numeric value to magic does not mean that it is not playing a powerful role at Disney and in other companies around the world. In fact, it is easy to see the effects of magic on business, particularly at a place like Walt Disney World. Just watch the guests. Observe the toddler whose turn has come to meet Mickey Mouse, life-size and in person; the teenager who has just emerged from The Twilight Zone Tower of Terror's thirteen-story free fall; or the parents who get back to the hotel after a long day and find a Winnie the Pooh plush doll with cookies and milk patiently waiting on the bed for their child. Each is a magic moment in which the bond between customer and company is forged and strengthened. And each contributes another small boost to Walt Disney World's return customer rate of around 70 percent.

But the effects of magic are not restricted to the theme park resorts. They are equally visible in the eyes of moviegoers as they watch films created at Disney subsidiary Pixar Animation Studios—films such as *Toy Story 3*, *Up*, and *WALL-E*, which won the Academy Award for Best Animated Feature in 2008. And in the smiles of shoppers as they interact with cast members in Disney's flagship store in Times Square in New York City. They can be heard in the yells of passengers riding the unique AquaDuck onboard water coaster on the Disney Cruise Lines' newest ship, the *Disney Dream*. And in cheers and groans of the millions of football fans who gather together to watch *Monday Night Football* on ESPN.

This kind of magic has a quality that leads to superior organizational performance. Each magical moment builds guest satisfaction and increases brand loyalty—and these are fundamental sources of organizational growth and success.

But think about a magic show. To the audience, the show elicits feelings of wonder and surprise. Most of those watching have no idea how the magician is creating the effects they are witnessing on the stage. Not knowing how an illusion is created and simply enjoying the show are a big part of the fun. The magician's perspective is completely different. To the magician, the show is a highly practical process made up of a series of meticulously planned, well-rehearsed steps that are designed to delight the audience.

This is true at The Walt Disney Company and at all other organizations that create magical customer experiences—whether the customers are consumers, tourists, patients, students, or other organizations. The happy surprise that a well-served customer feels is a result of hard work on the part of the organization and its employees. For the customer, the magic is a source of wonder and enjoyment. For the organization, magic is a much more practical matter.

"Disney really has practical magic figured out. Not that we get it perfect every time, but we come very, very close a lot of the time," explained Michael Eisner in *Harvard Business*

Review in 2000. "You can go anywhere in the world and see that in action. Go visit Animal Kingdom in Orlando or take one of our cruise ships to the Disney island, Castaway Cay. If you look at people's faces, you'll see that Disney still knows how to sweep people off their feet, out of their busy or stress-filled lives, and into experiences filled with wonder and excitement."[4]

For years, Disney cast members talked of "sprinkling pixie dust" to create magical experiences for their guests. But there is no line item for pixie dust on any Disney expense report. The pixie dust is the show that has been created—a show that runs at the Disney parks from the moment guests arrive until they leave for home.

In this book, as in the opening sequence of *The Wonderful World of Disney* that so many of us watched on television on the Sunday nights of our youths, we will pull back the curtain and take a look at the making of Disney's practical magic. We will explore how the company has been able to set a world-class benchmark for magical service, what the main ingredients of its pixie dust really are, and, most important, how you can create your own brand of practical magic in your organization.

MAGIC IN YOUR ORGANIZATION

Chances are very good that you are not working for a theme park or a movie studio or a sports network. Perhaps your company makes components for airplanes or sells business-to-business software online. Or perhaps you aren't in business at all. You may work in a school, not-for-profit hospital, or government agency. Perhaps, at first glance, Disney's magic does not seem to have a place in those types of organizations. Perhaps it is time to broaden your perspective.

Clearly, all organizations need customer-friendly employees. In fact, the number-one question that Disney Institute's corporate clientele asks us is "Can you make our people nice?" But Disney has much more in common with other organizations, large and small. Disney Institute facilitators and consultants use a simple exercise to help guests (in this case, the hundreds of thousands of people from more than thirty-five countries and forty industries who have attended Disney Institute programs) understand how similar Disney actually is to their own organizations. What, they ask, are the challenges your organizations are facing? The answers usually come fast and furious: the economic cycle, increased competition, a dearth of well-qualified job applicants, learning to partner effectively, customer satisfaction, and so on. It is a familiar list. Disney, the facilitators respond, faces the exact same challenges:

- Economic downturns constrain spending and can threaten the very survival of organizations. This is especially true in industry segments such as media, which relies on advertising and subscription fees, and entertainment, which relies on the discretionary spending of consumers. Disney's businesses are located squarely in those segments.

- Success breeds competition, and the competition is as hot as ever. In the theme park business, for example, one rival to Walt Disney World invested over $1 billion in 2009 and 2010. Nor is Walt Disney World's competition restricted to theme park operators: when executives from Harley-Davidson, Inc. attended programs at Disney Institute, they suggested that their company was a Disney competitor because both companies vie for consumers' discretionary income.

- No organization can succeed without a great workforce. The Walt Disney Company employs almost 150,000 people worldwide. Walt Disney World alone employs 62,000 people, who are working under ten collective bargaining agreements with thirty-two separate unions and in 1,500 different job classifications. Hiring, training, managing, and retaining such a large workforce is a huge undertaking.

- No organization can go it alone these days. The need to provide guests with an ever-greater diversity of products, services, and experiences has led The Walt Disney Company to seek out new partners around the world. Working effectively with such partners is essential in order to maintain Disney standards and brands, as well as business results.

- Finally, there is the classic service conundrum. Customer retention requires customer satisfaction, but customer satisfaction is a moving target. Customers as a whole are more demanding than ever before, and rightly so.

Further, delighting the repeat guests on whom The Walt Disney Company depends for its future success means that the company must raise the bar at every customer touch point.

The average organization has more in common with Disney than just business challenges. Underneath the trappings of every organization, we are all driving toward the same goal: serving the people who purchase and use our products and services. We all must satisfy our guests—and convince them to return and recommend us to others—or risk losing them in the long run.

Even manufacturing companies, which were traditionally product-focused, have come to the realization that they are also in the service business. In fact, there are service-based processes in every business. We take orders, create goods to suit specific needs, and deliver them according to the customer's instructions. Everyone is customer-facing—even if their customers are internal. Everyone needs to know how to create service magic.

Finally, as strange as this might sound, these days we are all in show business. In their influential Harvard Business School Press book *The Experience Economy*, B. Joseph Pine II and James Gilmore argued that we'd seen the demise of the Industrial Economy, which was focused solely on the efficient production of goods. Further, they said that we were past the peak of the Service Economy, which wrapped products in bundles of services to make them more attractive to customers.

Now, said the authors, we are in a new age of competition that they called the Experience Economy. Goods and services are simply props to engage the customer in this new era. Customers want memorable experiences, and companies must become stagers of experiences.

Here is the neat part. Pine and Gilmore described the ephemeral nature of experiences as follows: "However, while the *work* of the experience stager perishes upon its performance (precisely the right word), the *value* of the experience lingers in the memory of any individual who was engaged by the event." Sounds a lot like practical magic, doesn't it? They went on to use Disney as an example of a notable experience stager. "Most parents," they wrote, "don't take their kids to Walt Disney World just for the event itself but rather to make the shared experience part of the everyday family conversation for months, and even years, afterward."[5]

It is easy to picture Walt Disney nodding in agreement with these ideas. As we'll discuss in more depth later, when Walt threw his energies into the creation of Disneyland in the early 1950s, he was totally concentrated on the guest experience. In fact, the very idea for Disneyland was germinated during the Saturday trips to amusement parks that Walt made with his two daughters. In those days, amusement parks were slightly disreputable and often dirty and in poor condition. While he waited for his daughters to finish their rides, the successful animator began to watch the other customers and how they reacted to the parks. He asked himself, how could this experience be improved for the entire family?

Walt's answer was to create a new kind of amusement park, and since that beginning, Disneyland and all of the company's theme parks have been intensely focused on the guest experience. When you talk to Disney cast members about the parks, you will hear them described as "living movies," movies in which the guests themselves participate. As if no more elaboration was needed, Walt himself simply said, "Disneyland is a show."[6] With the infusion of some practical magic, your business could be, too.

DEFINING PRACTICAL MAGIC

The Disney theme parks and their many cast members make a clear distinction between being onstage and offstage. In Disney-speak, cast members are onstage whenever they are in the public areas of the parks and in front of guests. They are offstage when they are behind the scenes and out of their guests' sight.

Practical magic also has its onstage and offstage components. In this case, the onstage component of practical magic is the response that it produces in guests when everything comes together into a seamless, seemingly effortless performance. The offstage, or backstage, component is comprised of the nuts and bolts of creating practical magic. It includes all of the operations that add up to onstage magic. We are going to spend most of this book exploring that offstage component, which Disney calls Quality Service. To push the theater metaphor one step further, you can think of practical magic as the stage name for

Quality Service, the less-glitzy given name for the work that produces the magic.

Before we explore the components of service at Disney and how they come together, we should be clear about what we mean by Quality Service. Happily, it is a jargon-free, easy-to-understand definition: *Quality Service means exceeding your guests' expectations by paying attention to every detail of the delivery of your products and services.*

If this definition seems less than astounding, think about how you feel when you learn how a magic trick is accomplished. Suddenly, it all seems so simple. Like a magic show, there is no mystical incantation behind Disney's success, and anyone can learn and adapt the company's formula for practical magic. The challenge comes from living up to the two requirements of the Quality Service definition. That is much more difficult.

The Wow Factor

There is one thing that every guest brings when they visit Disney theme parks and purchase Disney products—expectations, often very high expectations. "Wowing" guests, to borrow a word from Tom Peters, means not only meeting these preconceived notions of what a Disney vacation or film or toy should be, but *exceeding* them. In the same way, you must first meet and then exceed the expectations of your customers if you are going to build a reputation for Quality Service.

Many companies wow their customers on occasion. An employee goes above and beyond the call of duty, solves a problem, and earns some high-profile gratitude from a customer. Maybe that employee will get a premium parking spot for a month or a certificate for pizza. The story will be told and retold and will perhaps be added to corporate lore—but then it's back to business as usual.

At Disney, exceeding guests' expectations is the standard call of duty. If you study the Disney theme parks, you can see how that works on myriad occasions each day. It shows up in the willingness of a restaurant hostess to not only provide directions when you are lost but to leave her post to guide you to your destination. It appears at the end of some late-night shopping when the cashier takes the time to find out who you are and where you are staying and then recommends the free boat ride back to your hotel and offers a map to the dock. In Disney Institute programs, facilitators are not surprised as they listen to their guests tell stories like these each morning. "That's the cast's job," is their pithy response. In fact, it is this plethora of little wows, many of which seem fairly insignificant at the time, on which Quality Service depends. If the little wows are delivered consistently and continuously, they add up to a big WOW!

As we will see, superlative face-to-face service is just one element in the work of exceeding guest expectations. It means paying close attention to every aspect of the guest experience. It means analyzing that experience from the guest's perspective, understanding the needs and wants of the guest, and committing every element of the business—from the design of each element of the infrastructure to the interaction between guest and cast—to the creation of an exceptional experience.

Bumping the Lamp

There is a corporate-wide obsession to detail at Disney. Walt was famous for his eye for detail, and he made sure that everyone paid the same attention that he did.

The seeds of the company's obsession were planted during its early years, when its only business was the making of animated films. Animation by hand remains a rigorous art today. Twenty-four frames per second, each a still portrait of that fractional moment, must come together to create an entire story, a complete world designed and populated with characters. The ability to capture the minds and emotions of the audience members is entirely dependent on the depth and consistency of the animator's vision. There is no famous actor to carry the weight, no spectacular natural setting.

Walt brought the attention to detail inherent in the animator's art to all of his company's ventures, and that tradition carries through to the present day. It has been referred to as "bumping the lamp."

Bumping the lamp was born during the filming of the Walt Disney Pictures film *Who Framed Roger Rabbit*. The film was an innovative mix of live action and animation. In one scene, the movie's leading man, Bob Hoskins, bumps into a lamp hanging from the ceiling. The lamp swings back and forth, and so does its shadow. During the making of the film, the lamp and its shadow appeared in the live-action setting the same way it would in the natural world. But what happened when the animated star, Roger Rabbit, was added to the scene? That's right—no shadow crossed our wisecracking hero's face.

Most of the film's viewers would not notice the difference, and certainly the scene could have been shot without Hoskins bumping into the lamp. But the film's animation artists made sure that the shading on Roger Rabbit accurately reflected the moving shadow cast by the live-action lamp in each of the twenty-four frames in every second of the scene. They paid attention to the details and took that extra step in their commitment to a quality guest experience.

A more recent example of bumping the lamp can be found in a scene in *WALL-E*, a Pixar film about a lonely little robot who is left behind to clean up Earth after humans have abandoned the planet. Nearly six miles of cityscape were designed and built in a computer to make WALL-E's world believable to audiences. WALL-E is a collector; in one scene, he returns to his home after a day's work, and the audience sees this firsthand. In this single scene, Pixar's animators populated WALL-E's home with 827 poker chips, sixty-six license plates, 290 fake eyeballs, etc. The lighting sources in his home include 798 Christmas lights, two cords of forty-eight chili lights, four bug zappers, five paper lanterns, and ten tiki lights. No viewer could possibly see all of these items. So why did Pixar include them? "It's the little *whispers* that speak to an audience," explained director Andrew Stanton.

The attention to detail in our other businesses is just as intense. On the *Disney Magic*, a ship in the Disney Cruise Line fleet, it can be seen in the magic portholes in the inside cabins. These portholes are actually LCD flat-screen monitors that are connected to high-definition cameras. The cameras transmit—in real time—the same view you would see if you looked out of a real porthole. In addition, just to bump the lamp a bit, you might also see a pirate ship or a Disney character floating by. At Walt Disney World, you'll see the attention to every detail in the hotel room doors that have two peepholes, one at the usual height and one at a child's-eye level. You'll see it also in the planning that goes into the intervals between trash cans—the park's designers figured out exactly how far an average person would carry a piece of trash before pitching it (about twenty-seven feet) and then factored that into crowd densities. Take a quick survey of those trash cans as you move from one area of the Magic Kingdom to another. You will also see that their design changes to reflect each area's theme.

Exceeding guests' expectations is Disney's service strategy, and paying attention to every detail is the tactic by which it is accomplished. They are inextricably interwoven tasks. In attending to the details, Disney consistently exceeds the expectations of the guest. Perhaps, like the changing appearance of the trash cans, they are never consciously noticed at all—the guests' attention is simply never interrupted by something that doesn't look like it should be there. When the experience is consistent, seamless, and of high quality, guests return. And when they do, they come with heightened expectations, which, in turn, incite Disney to even greater attention to detail.

Exceeding expectations by attending to the details is how you can create practical magic for your customers, but it is not, in and of itself, sufficient to drive the day-to-day work of Quality Service. We can simply command everyone in our companies to bump the lamp and wow guests, but the results will surely leave something to be desired. There is a good chance that go-getters on your staff will take off running in opposite directions implementing their own versions of Quality Service, and the rest will shift around uneasily and finally ask, how exactly are we expected to do that?

That question, which is entirely logical, is answered with Disney's Quality Service Compass. This compass encapsulates the organization-wide model that generates Quality Service. It is the production process through which practical magic is created. In its essence, the compass can be used to create a shared vision of service that aligns the major elements that every organization shares—its people, infrastructure, and processes—in a cohesive, comprehensive effort to deliver that vision.

The body of this book is devoted to exploring how the points of the compass work and how they are applied within Disney as well as in a variety of other organizations, commercial and institutional, that have used Disney Institute as a source of ideas and concepts for creating their own service strategies.

THE QUALITY SERVICE COMPASS

The Quality Service Compass has four main points: guestology, quality standards, delivery systems, and integration. Our service objective—to exceed guest expectations—resides at the center of the compass.

Compass Point 1: Guestology

Guestology is what Disney calls the art and science of knowing and understanding customers. It is the first point on the compass because the needs, wants, perceptions, and emotions of guests are the basis for the action that takes place in all of the other points. Guestology establishes an initial course of action, and as new customer information is gathered, that data is used to fine-tune and improve performance.

Guestology enables organizations to provide a context for their service strategies. In what sense does Disney seek to exceed guest expectations? We don't try to provide the least expensive products and services; we want to provide high-quality entertainment. Nor do we try to provide the fastest service; we could eliminate wait times in our parks by speeding up the rides, but in many cases, that would ruin the fun. The context within which we seek to exceed expectations is happiness. *At Disney, we try to create happiness for people of all ages everywhere.* This common purpose is a rallying flag. It aligns the efforts of cast members and establishes a foundation for their own behavior toward guests. For management, making guests happier than they expected to be is a guiding precept. Every decision can be measured against it. Whether a decision supports the common purpose is an important managerial litmus test.

Compass Point 2: Quality Standards

Once you have defined your service goals, you can begin to consider *quality standards*, the second point on the Quality Service Compass. Quality standards serve two purposes: they establish the criteria for actions that are necessary to accomplish the service strategy, and they serve as the measures of Quality Service. At the Disney resorts and parks, there are four quality standards. In order of importance, they are *safety, courtesy, show,* and *efficiency.* As we'll see later, they are ordered in strict priority, which further guides the efforts of cast members and helps facilitate decision-making at the parks.

Every business will have a unique common purpose and its own quality standards. In Chapter 2, we will explore how these are created and used at both Disney and at a variety of other organizations, and we'll discuss the basic tools and techniques of guestology.

Compass Point 3: Delivery Systems

With a common purpose and quality standards in place, we move to the next point in the Quality Service Compass—delivery systems. There are three service-delivery systems that all companies share: their employees, their setting, and their processes. Each is explored, in turn, in chapters 3, 4, and 5.

Cast: In the past few decades, organizations everywhere have begun to understand that their employees are their most important asset. This is particularly true in the delivery of Quality Service. Often, employees are on the front lines, face-to-face with customers. And even when they are not in direct contact with customers, they are controlling the operation of the processes by which service is delivered. For example, the Disney theme parks have been measuring the impact of cast on the guest experience for more than fifty years. What is one of the most-often stated reasons why guests return for another visit? The cast.

"Disney Imagineers go to great lengths to make the theme parks feel intimate, but it's the cast members who really make it work," says Jeff James, Vice President, Disney Institute. "A $200 million attraction won't be fun if the cast member at the front is less than pleasant."[7] This statement and the results behind it would have surely resonated with Walt. After all, a friendly, approachable, and helpful cast was an important element in his vision for a new kind of amusement park from the outset.

Preparing the cast to deliver Quality Service is an essential task that starts with the introduction and dissemination of a generic, organization-wide set of image and behavioral standards. At Disney, every new cast member learns these *performance tips* during their first on-the-job experience, the Disney Traditions orientation program. One aspect of this training that you have already been exposed to is its language. The very words that are used to describe customers, work, employees, and so on suggest the way in which cast members will be expected to approach their roles.

As in other organizations, Disney's 150,000 cast members play a huge number of different roles. So a large part of the work of equipping the cast with the information and tools they need must be conducted on the job. This requires the creation of location-specific *performance cultures*. A performance culture is a set of behaviors, mannerisms, terms, and values that are taught to new cast members as they enter their job location.

As we will see in Chapter 3, the generic performance tips that define behavior across the organization and the job-specific performance culture are both used to build the skills and talent of the cast. They also provide a baseline for evaluation and improvement.

Setting: The second service-delivery system is the setting in which you conduct business. Your setting is wherever your customers meet you. Whether that is a retail store or a hospital or a Web site or a telephone call center, the setting that customers encounter plays a critical role in how they perceive their experience with your organization. The importance of managing the effect of setting on the guest experience can be summed up in two words: *Everything speaks.*

Here's a quick example from Disney's history. John Hench, one of the original Disney Imagineers (the folks who design and build all of Disney's theme parks), remembers watching Walt finesse a setting: "I was so astonished by the way Walt would create a kind of live-action cross-dissolve when passing from one area of Disneyland to another. He would even insist on changing the texture of the pavement at the threshold of each new land because, he said, 'You can get information about a changing environment through the soles of your feet.'"[8]

In Disney theme parks, "everything speaks" means that every detail—from the doorknobs to the dining rooms—sends a message to guests. That message must be consistent with the common purpose and quality standards, and it must support and further the show being created. The next time you are in the Magic Kingdom, have some fun and pay attention to what your feet sense as you walk from one themed area to the next.

Setting includes the environment, the objects located within the environment, and the procedures that enhance the quality of the environment. We will be exploring several specific ways to work with setting in Chapter 4: we will see how setting can incorporate quality standards, how it can guide the guest experience, and how it can speak to all of a guest's senses.

Process: The third service-delivery system is process. Processes often encompass and utilize both cast and setting, and they comprise the most prominent service-delivery system in most organizations. At Disney theme parks, service processes include moving guests through the attractions, the check-in and checkout processes at the hotels, and the response to emergencies, such as medical problems and fires.

There are combustion points in every process. These are spots where even a finely tuned process can break down (especially when several hundred thousand guests are straining its capacity) and, instead of contributing to a positive customer experience, begin to turn a guest's good day into a bad one. It's impossible to completely eliminate combustion points, but the goal is to stop them from turning into explosion points.

One example Disney facilitators like to use involves a common parking problem. After a long day of fun, guests often forget where they left their car. The lots are labeled, the rows are numbered, and the trams that shuttle guests to the entrance announce the parking location several times, but inevitably and regularly cars are misplaced.

Instead of leaving tired guests forlorn and wandering, members of the parking lot cast came up with a service patch. Since the parking lots are filled in order, the tram drivers started keeping a simple list of what row they were working at what time in the morning. The lists are copied and distributed to members of the parking cast at the end of the day, so if guests can remember about what time they arrived (which they usually can), a cast member can tell them about where they parked. Combustion point defused and service hero created!

Debugging, as identifying and solving the lost-car problem, is one of the process issues we will explore in more detail in

Chapter 5. We will also look at three other process-based issues that add quality to the guest experience: cast-to-guest communication, or how to ensure the cast can solve guest problems; guest flow, or "How long is that line?"; and service attention, or how to handle guests who cannot utilize a service process.

Compass Point 4: Integration

The last point in the Quality Service Compass is integration. Integration means quite simply that the three delivery systems are combined and aligned to create a complete operating system. Cast, setting, and process are merged in pursuit of the service strategy. The result: an exceptionally high-quality guest experience that drives the success of all organizations known for service excellence.

Integration is a logical, step-by-step process. In Chapter 6, we will describe an easily adapted matrix that you can use as a guide to successfully achieve integration in your organization. The Integration Matrix not only serves as a battle plan for attaining Quality Service, but it can also be used to troubleshoot service problems and benchmark the practices of other organizations, including Disney.

CHAPTER 2

The Magic of Service

In 1928, Mickey Mouse stormed the box office, and he has since become a global icon. The cartoon mouse, born of the imagination and voice of Walt Disney and the artistry of Ub Iwerks—the first in a long line of Disney animation masters—was not, however, an instant star. Even though Walt was offering up the first cartoon with a sound track, he could not find a film distributor who was willing to bring Mickey to theaters.

It was a New York City theater operator and promoter named Harry Reichenbach who finally offered Walt a solution. "Those guys don't know what's good until the public tells them," said Reichenbach of the distributors. He convinced Walt to show *Steamboat Willie* in his theater for two weeks. Mickey was a hit with moviegoers, and, just as Reichenbach had predicted, the distributors flocked to sign up Disney and its mouse.

Walt had learned an important lesson about the power of Disney's audience. When he tried to launch *The Skeleton Dance*, the first of the studio's innovative *Silly Symphony* cartoons in 1929, the distributors rejected him once more. This time, they wanted "more mice." So he went directly to the audience, and their acceptance again powered a distribution deal. Again, in 1948, when Walt had trouble finding distribution support for *Seal Island*, the first of Disney's nature/adventure films, he went to the audience for the help he needed. And he got it.[1]

Pick a group of people in any major urban area around the world and ask them about Walt. They will invariably associate the man with an animated character, a movie, or a theme park. But Walt should be just as famous for his achievements as a guestologist. Although Walt was a master at knowing and understanding customers, he certainly never heard of service concepts such as "customer-focus," "close to the customer," and "customer-centric." Yet in his straightforward, Midwestern way, Walt clearly understood that customers were the most important—and the final—judges of the entertainment produced at his company.

"We are not trying to entertain the critics," he would say. "I'll take my chances with the public."[2] But like all the best guestologists, Walt was usually not taking much of a chance. Invariably, he had already polled the opinions of the company's customers and had included their advice in the refinement of his ideas.

Popular actor Kurt Russell, who spent his teen years making live-action movies for Disney, was surprised by the attention the head of studio paid to him. "Sometimes he'd come down to the set and ask, 'Do you want to see a part of the movie that's being put together?' So I'd watch a movie or parts of a movie with him and we'd talk about it and he'd ask me questions," recalls Kurt. "What was interesting about Walt, as I look back on it now, is that he was picking the mind of an uninhibited thirteen-year-old. He would ask, 'What do you think of this?' and we'd kick ideas back and forth. I think he was finding out how a young mind worked."[3]

Walt's drive to find out what and how an audience thought extended into Disneyland. The next time you walk through the arched entry tunnels of Disneyland and emerge into Main Street, U.S.A., look to your left at the Fire Station, which is located next to City Hall, overlooking the Town Square. If you examine its facade, you will see a lamp burning in one of the second-story windows. The light is a tribute to Walt; it illuminates the small apartment that he used as his headquarters while overseeing the construction of the park and its early days of operation. From the window of that apartment, Walt watched Disneyland's guests as they got their first impressions of the park.

If the image of Walt peering out above the crowd gives you the idea that he was shy about face-to-face encounters with guests, nothing could be further from the truth. Walt not only reveled in sharing the experience of Disneyland, he made a regular practice of wandering the park collecting the responses of guests.

Tony Baxter, who eventually became Senior Vice President

at Walt Disney Imagineering and served as the executive designer of Disneyland Paris, had various jobs at Disneyland as a teenager. He would bring his younger sister to the park with him, and she would play while he worked. One day, his sister and a friend saw Walt in the park and followed him to It's a Small World. The three of them rode through the attraction, and when it was over, Walt asked if they liked it enough to do it again. Yes, came the answer. Walt replied, "Then you need to sing the song this time," and the trio—two children and the leader of a corporate empire—took a second trip.[4]

When it was suggested that an administration building be erected for the management at Disneyland, Walt was vehemently opposed. "I don't want you guys sitting behind desks. I want you out in the park, watching what people are doing and finding out how you can make the place more enjoyable for them."[5] When he found that the staff was leaving the property to eat, Walt steamed, "Stand in line with the people, and for god's sake, don't go off the lot to eat like you guys have been doing. You eat at the park and listen to people!"[6]

> *In my organization there is respect for every individual, and we all have a keen respect for the public.*
> —Walt Disney

The most impressive result of Walt's spirited emphasis on knowing and understanding customers is Walt Disney World itself. In the late 1950s, Walt was already planning a new park somewhere in the eastern half of the United States, but he was not 100 percent sure that a Disneyland-style park would appeal to the citizens of the East Coast. The 1964 World's Fair in New York gave him the perfect opportunity to test his unique brand of entertainment using someone else's money and the biggest focus group ever assembled—the tens of millions of people who attended the fair in 1964 and 1965. Walt corralled the sponsors, and WED Enterprises—which would later become Walt Disney Imagineering—created four major attractions, including It's a Small World for Pepsi-Cola. By the time the fair closed, it was estimated that fifty million people had seen at least one of the four Disney attractions, which were acclaimed as the most popular. And Walt was sure that there was a huge East Coast audience for a new Disney park.

Guestology is just as important at Disney today. For instance, Disney licensed its characters and brands to baby product companies for many years, establishing consumer interest in the Disney brand. Then Disney Consumer Products established its own baby product business, Disney Baby. In early 2011, Disney Baby began testing a new line of baby apparel by partnering with Our365, a company that sells bedside baby pictures of newborns and delivers free gift baskets to new parents. Disney Baby gave away more than two hundred thousand bodysuits for newborns in this marketing program. And if new parents like the bodysuits, Disney Baby will extend its apparel lines and eventually expand into other products, such as bath items, strollers, baby food, etc.

GUESTOLOGY REVEALED

Since guestology sounds somewhat mysterious, let's pull back the curtain a bit. *Guestology* is Disney-speak for market and customer research needed to learn who guests are and understand what they expect from your organization. The time and effort that Disney devotes to guestology demonstrates how important we believe it is to the ultimate success of our company and, for that matter, any organization that undertakes the Quality Service journey.

At Walt Disney World, for example, the guestology budget is invested in a whole slew of techniques, some of which your organization probably also uses. There are face-to-face surveys conducted on the property, typically at the park gates and other main access points. Specific "listening posts" are created as dedicated locations to answer guest questions, solve problems, and collect information. Comment cards are as common as smiles, and, perhaps most important, cast members throughout the resort collect and report the opinions and observations of guests as a standard part of their jobs.

Utilization studies, too, contribute to the Walt Disney World guestology database. Usage and visitation patterns at the resort are analyzed and compared. Do guests typically visit Pirates of the Caribbean early or late in the day? How many guests use the resort's transportation systems each hour? What are the occupancy rates at the various resorts? Such studies are all part of the Quality Service brew.

Mystery shoppers make purchases to verify the service in the resort's many stores and gift shops. Telephone surveys are used to develop information from both random population samples and recent guests. Guest letters and e-mails are studied for more clues to improving service. And focus groups are used to gather information for future development and the refinement of the existing rides and attractions.

A Disney Institute training client, Cherie Barnett, made good use of focus groups in the expansion of her Michigan-based chain of hair emporiums, Glitz Salons. When an industry statistic pinpointed girls between the ages of ten and sixteen as the largest consumers of cosmetics, Ms. Barnett started thinking about a hair salon targeted directly at that niche market. The first thing she did was reach out to her potential audience.

"I got on the phone and asked them to come to my house and talk to me about this. Grabbed kids from the region—bring your friends, don't bring Mom," recalls the entrepreneur. "I worked with groups of twenty to twenty-five at a time. I asked them to tell me what they wanted in a salon—what music, decorations, logo. The ideas and how their minds worked were incredible. They actually created the logo; I just took it to the marketing people and said, 'make it.'" The result was Glitz NXT, which became the third salon in the privately held chain.

> *You don't build it for yourself. You know what people want, and you build it for them.*
> —Walt Disney

Information developed by guestology techniques is utilized in many ways. Obviously, there is no point in investing a single cent in market research if the findings are hidden away in a desk drawer. The knowledge developed from guests must be used to create and improve all the points of the Quality Service Compass, from the service standards to the smallest details of the service-delivery systems of cast, setting, and process. The major applications of customer data are to establish a baseline and other criteria for the development and implementation of the service strategy and to create improvements and other adjustments to the existing service plan. Disney uses guest input for all these purposes.

Smart guestologists also realize that their customers—and their expectations—are changing all the time. Thus, guestology is an ongoing task. Surveys must be made regularly to be useful. Certainly, our guests at Walt Disney World have changed over the years. A survey conducted among our guests when the park opened in 1971 would be of use only as a historical document today. Fundamental guest demographics, such as size and composition of the average party as well as guest attitudes and expectations, have shifted, and they will shift again. Guestology helps track the ever-changing guest landscape and offers the cues needed to adjust our service delivery.

Customer responses change over the short term as well as the long term. Guests just arriving back in port after a Disney Cruise vacation will feel differently than guests whose credit card statement has arrived after thirty days back at home. To create a magical service experience, Disney needs to know how their guests feel across a broad spectrum of time. For these reasons, it is critical to gather information at a variety of points before, during, and after the guest's experience.

At Walt Disney World, we know that guests have encounters with cast members many times during their stay. Each can be an opportunity for the cast member to learn more about guests, improve the show, and build a stronger bond between Disney and its guests. We will explore how this is accomplished in the next chapter.

KNOWING AND UNDERSTANDING GUESTS

When we say that guestology is the science of knowing and understanding guests, we are also defining the two major kinds of information developed by guest research. These are *demographic* and *psychographic*.

Demographics

At Disney, demographic information is thought of as factual knowledge about our guests. Demographics mainly describe the physical attributes of a group and often comprise quantitative data. Demographic information reveals who customers are, where they come from, how much effort they expend to get here, how much money they spend, etc.

Another valuable aspect of demographics is that when you know who your guests are, you automatically know who your guests are *not*. Figuring out who is *not* doing business with you sometimes triggers huge changes in service theme and strategies, especially if you find that you are missing a large group of potential customers.

Demographics help us ensure that the Quality Service

Compass is correctly centered. This may all seem pretty elementary, but it is surprising how often demographics open an organization's eyes to basic marketplace realities that have been overlooked.

Psychographics

Psychographic information is the category of customer research data that helps Disney understand its guests' mental states. Pyschographics offer clues to what customers need, what they want, what preconceived notions they bring to the table, and what emotions they experience. At Disney Institute, we categorize these clues as needs, wants, stereotypes, and emotions, and we can create a new compass model—called the Guestology Compass—to express them.

THE MAGIC OF SERVICE

Developing the four points of the Guestology Compass means generating qualitative responses from customers. This is done by asking open-ended questions and encouraging customers to speak their minds. The answers add up to a portrait of guest expectations, which in turn becomes the baseline for the work of exceeding those expectations.

Let's take a closer look at the elements of the Guestology Compass with the help of two examples, Walt Disney World and BMW Canada, Inc. BMW Canada, which has sent more than seven hundred of its retail center personnel to Disney Institute training, was established in 1986 as a wholly owned subsidiary of Munich-based BMW AG, and it manages a network of sixty-five BMW and MINI automobile retailers and nineteen motorcycle retailers across Canada.

Needs are the easiest of the four compass points to determine. What do guests need when they come to Walt Disney World? A vacation. What do they need when they go to a BMW retail center? A car. Needs tend to be obvious, usually corresponding to the products and services you offer, but they only provide the rough outline of a psychographic profile.

Wants are less obvious. They suggest a customer's deeper purpose. Many of Walt Disney World's guests want more than a simple vacation; they also want long-lived memories of a fun-filled family experience. BMW's customer may want the status of a high-performance car. As you begin to uncover wants, the contours of the customer profile take shape, which may cut across demographics, geographies, and other traditional marketing approaches.

Stereotypes are those preconceived notions that every customer has of your business or industry. Guests come to Disney's parks expecting the cast members to treat them a certain way. At the BMW dealership, customers will expect the technicians to treat them a certain way. As you identify guest stereotypes, you obtain valuable clues about their expectations. These clues help us fill in the features of the guest portrait.

Finally, *emotions* are the feelings that customers experience throughout their contact with your organization. At Walt Disney World, guests are likely to have a wide range of emotions during their visit. Some are positive, such as the excitement of riding the Rock 'n' Roller Coaster, and some are negative, such as impatience with long lines. At BMW, car buyers experience a similar range of emotions. They may feel proud and excited driving off in their new cars and apprehensive returning for their first service visits. The goal of both businesses is to create a positive emotional connection even when customers are actually deducting the cost of their purchase from their bank accounts. (How many of your customers still say "wow" *after* making payment?) Identifying the changing emotional state of customers completes the coloration of the profile.

The following table offers several more examples of the customer profiles developed in the guestology process. As you examine it, think about what a profile of your customers would look like.

At Disney, the process of collecting and analyzing the data required to complete the Guestology Compass goes a long way toward understanding what guests expect from our products, services, and experiences. This knowledge is used to fulfill and exceed guest expectations at the remaining points in the Quality Service Compass.

THE POWER OF A COMMON PURPOSE

"My business is making people, especially children, happy," Walt Disney said half a century ago.[7] Although it is a simple and direct statement on the surface, Walt's quote plumbs the depths of The Walt Disney Company's service ethic. It is the basis for our mission as a business; it represents what we stand for and why we exist. It is our *common purpose.*

In 1955, as Walt's vision of Disneyland became a reality, that purpose was first made manifest as a way to introduce the new park's first employees to the basics of Disney service and to guide them in their interactions with guests. In the first Disney University orientation classes, it was called a "common goal," and the cast was taught *We'll create happiness.* There has been an alteration or two over the years, but today's new cast members hear essentially the same message. Today, they are taught *We create happiness by providing the finest in entertainment for people of all ages, everywhere.*

There has been a great deal of talk about organizational vision, mission, and values in the business world since the 1950s. Management thinkers have identified these statements of organizational intent as highly effective workplace unifiers and have shown in studies that companies with well-defined ideologies are successful in the long-term. Jim Collins and

BE OUR GUEST

	Needs	Wants
Walt Disney World Resort	Vacation	Happiness Lasting memories
Insurance Agency	Life insurance policy	Peace of mind
Automobile Dealer	Car	Status Freedom Reliability
Financial Institution	Bank account	Financial security Investment returns

THE MAGIC OF SERVICE

Stereotypes	Emotions
Disney is for kids	Excitement entering the
Long lines	park
Clean	Tired feet at the end of
Friendly	the day
Expensive	Thrill of Space Mountain
Fun	
You never get your money back	Uncertainty of whether you're covered when an
Like a neighbor who is there when you need help	emergency occurs
	Relief when you're covered
Takes forever to get paid on a claim	
Used-car salesman	The excitement of buying
New-car salesman	a car
Luxury-car salesman	Buyer's remorse several days later
Marble floor	Impatience over long lines
Wool suits and oxford shirts	at drive-up teller
	Excitement as you close a
Bankers' hours	loan on your first home
Long waits for tellers	

Jerry Porras, the authors of *Built to Last*, called them Visionary Companies and found that they "outperformed the general stock market by a factor of 12 since 1925."

"Leaders die, products become obsolete, markets change, new technologies emerge, and management fads come and go, but core ideology in a great company endures as a source of guidance and inspiration," they wrote in *Harvard Business Review*.[8]

Many organizations got the message and quickly created statements regarding their purpose and values. They engraved them on plaques and hung them for everyone, customers and employees, to see. And in many cases, that was about as far as the effort went; a well-chosen sentiment to which no one paid much attention. Collins and Porras say that this is because the core ideology (the purpose and values of an organization) is not something that can be simply declared. Instead, it must either reflect existing truths about a company or create new ideals that will be pursued until they become inherent truths.

Like that of companies such as Johnson & Johnson, 3M, and Hewlett-Packard, Disney's common purpose is successful because it is deeply rooted in its heritage and supported throughout the day-to-day operations of the business. It is a *living* theme, not just a sentence on a plaque, and it serves three critical needs: it clearly defines the organization's mission, it communicates a message internally, and it creates an image of the organization.

Loud and clear, Disney's common purpose declares a goal (*to create happiness*), states how that goal is to be accomplished (*by providing the finest in entertainment*), and defines a customer base (*people of all ages, everywhere*). Today, "entertainment" at Disney means television, films, books, theme parks, cruises, toys, etc. But its common purpose creates a clear focus on what and what is not appropriate for our company. You will probably never see a Disney-made jet or get a home loan at the Bank of Disney. A common purpose defines an organization's boundaries.

A common purpose also communicates its message throughout the organization. It relates an ultimate goal to every one of the 150,000 people who work at Disney worldwide and serves as a rallying point across the organization. It is one thing that all cast members have in common and no matter what the individual job, it defines the expectation that all of us will help create happiness for our guests.

Finally, a common purpose theme creates the foundation for the public image of the company. It tells our guests what they can expect to get from the company (*the finest in entertainment*). It is an explicit promise and a double-edged sword: if guests' expectations are met or exceeded, then they are happy. If not, their displeasure will be obvious.

Even if the words sound similar, every organization creates its own unique common purpose. Obviously, Disney's mission of creating happiness cannot simply be adopted and imitated: it is critical to create your own *service-oriented* purpose. It is a fundamental element in the Quality Service Compass.

Here's what Tom Peters and Bob Waterman had to say on the subject in their groundbreaking book, *In Search of*

Excellence: "Whether or not they are as fanatic in their service obsession as Frito, IBM, or Disney, the excellent companies all seem to have very powerful service themes that pervade the institutions. In fact, one of our most significant conclusions about the excellent companies is that, *whether their basic business is metal-bending, high technology, or hamburgers, they have all defined themselves as service businesses.*"[9]

The United States government spent most of the 1990s redefining itself as a service business. One of the principle tenets of this initiative, started during the Clinton Administration, required reorganizing governmental agencies as performance-based organizations (PBOs) that were customer-centric. The first officially mandated PBO was Student Financial Assistance (SFA) at the U.S. Department of Education. At the time, SFA, a Disney Institute client, processed more than $60 billion in grants, student loans, and work-study assistance each year. Its common purpose was simple and compelling: *We put America through school.*

With that short sentence SFA directly targeted its end customers, the more than nine million American students that it helped to pursue a higher education annually. It was a critical focus for the agency's employees because they did not always deal directly with the American families that needed student loans. Instead, they worked with partners—schools, banks, and loan guarantors, who acted as the delivery system to the ultimate customer, the student. The refocusing of employee attention on students was what the late Greg Woods, the CEO of SFA and leader of the reinvention effort, was talking about

The Evolution of the Disney Common Purpose

Year	Common Purpose	Meaning
1955	We'll create happiness.	At the outset of the idea of the theme parks, working from the film medium heritage, happiness was identified as the "want" the guests were in search of. The "we" was the cast members, as a team.
1971	We create happiness by providing the finest in family entertainment.	The introduction of the word "finest" acknowledged that there was a marketplace and competition in turbulent times.
1990	We create happiness by providing the finest in entertainment for people of all ages, everywhere.	By the nineties, Disney had recognized the huge diversity of the potential guest population in what was becoming a world market.
2011 and beyond	We create happiness . . .	Disney continues to monitor the changes and requirements of the guests. Even though the service theme continues to evolve, it, in some measure, remains the same.

when he said, "If the folks who work at SFA think their job is to make loans and grants, they take almost a mechanical approach to it, of moving paper from point A to point B. But if they're in touch with what it is they're really doing, they see they're helping people reach their dreams. Then they do a different job."[10]

It is worth noting that the first place the SFA went to learn how to better serve customers was to its customers. Woods formed a task force comprised of line personnel that conducted two hundred listening sessions with students, parents, and operating partners from around the nation. More than eight thousand customer comments were collected and analyzed *before* improvements were determined. That's guestology in practice.

A final note about common purpose: It need not be forever fixed. SFA, for example, now provides over $150 billion in new aid annually. In 2006, it changed its common purpose to "Start here. Go further." Nothing lasts forever. But we believe that when a purpose is properly established, it will change only very slowly, evolving over a long period of time.

In fact, Collins and Porras suggested that unlike a business strategy or set of goals, an organization's core purpose can and should last at least a century. "Whereas you might achieve a goal or complete a strategy, you cannot fulfill a purpose; it is like a guiding star on the horizon—forever pursued but never reached," they explained. "Yet although purpose itself does not change, it does inspire change. The very fact that purpose can never be fully realized means that an organization can never stop stimulating change and progress."[11] That is as good a summation of the power of a common purpose as you will find anywhere.

DEFINING THE COMMON PURPOSE

Since a common purpose acts as a promise to your customers and a mission for your employees, the next logical question is, How will you fulfill that promise and mission? The answer is the establishment of *quality standards*, the second point on the Quality Service Compass. Quality standards, or service values, are the operational criteria that ensure the consistent delivery of a common purpose. They flow from the organizational purpose and in turn, support its achievement.

At Disney, our quality standards are deeply rooted in the history of the company's attractions business. In the 1940s, when Walt first imagined Disneyland, they were an implicit part of his vision of an amusement park that would be wholly unlike the ones he had been taking his children to visit. Walt's park would be clean, its employees would be friendly, and every member of the family would be able to have fun in it. In 1955, when training consultant Van France and Dick Nunis, who later became Chairman of Walt Disney Attractions, created the orientation class for Disneyland's first employees, they worked from the "creating happiness" theme and started linking its achievement to specific behaviors. In 1962, when Dick refined those behaviors into the four components of a "good show," the park's quality standards were explicitly defined.

Dick's four elements were Safety, Courtesy, Show, and Capacity (which was later relabeled Efficiency), and today, they are still the quality standards for the Disney parks and resorts business. They represent how the common purpose is fulfilled and offer a set of filters that help Disney employees to judge and prioritize the actions that contribute to the guest experience. Let's take a closer look at how our quality standards support the common purpose.

Safety

It is a gross understatement to say that a guest who is injured or who feels insecure about his or her safety or the safety of loved ones is going to be unhappy. So the quality standard of safety requires that the welfare and peace of mind of our guests are always provided for.

Disney Imagineer Bruce Johnson explained what that means in the creation of attractions: "The statistics are very much against us. Think about it. If there is a one-in-a-million chance something will go wrong and ten million guests ride our ride, then something will happen ten times. We can't design to that one in a million. We have to design to one in hundreds of millions."[12]

By adopting safety as a quality standard, Disney ensures that safety concerns are addressed in every element of its resorts and parks. Safety features, often above and beyond local codes, are designed into the attractions, transport systems, hotels, and eateries. In addition to a large dedicated security staff, the entire cast resort-wide is taught safety procedures and location-specific safety practices.

Courtesy

The quality standard of courtesy requires that every guest be treated like a VIP—that is, a very important, very *individual* person. Fulfilling the standard means more than simply treating people the way we would want to be treated; it means treating them the way that *they* want to be treated, with recognition and respect for their emotions, abilities, and cultures.

Whether you live in Orlando, Florida, or in Hong Kong, all you have to do is ask for directions to figure out if someone works at Disney. If the person assisting you points using two or more fingers or an open hand, the odds are good that they work at the Mouse's House. That's because pointing with one finger is considered impolite in some cultures, and so one of the first things all new cast members are taught is how to point courteously.

Making courtesy a quality standard means turning it into a set of organization-wide behaviors. As an organization, it makes the Disney parks and resorts responsible for recruiting, hiring, and training a cast with great interpersonal skills. The cast is taught to take a wide responsibility for guest happiness by being friendly, knowing the answers to common questions, and, when possible, personally guiding guests to their destinations. For cast members, it means taking a proactive approach to courtesy by anticipating and reaching out to assist and engage

Disney's guests. As Disney Institute facilitators say, "Guests may not always be right, but they are always our guests."

Show

The quality standard of show requires that there be seamless and exceptional entertainment for guests. Disney's common purpose calls for the "finest in entertainment," and at its highest level, that means a performance that is uninterrupted from the beginning to the end of a guest's stay at the resort. The fact that the Disney theme parks are the most popular in the world is a testament to the pursuit of the standard of show.

Walt Disney was always focused on providing a good show, one in which the audience's attention was never unintentionally diverted or otherwise interrupted. Marty Sklar, the now-retired Chairman of Walt Disney Imagineering, remembered walking through Disneyland with Walt. As they reached the Mike Fink Keel Boats in Frontierland, a company publicist drove up to the pair. Walt was shocked. "What," he demanded, "are you doing with a car here in 1860?"[13]

Story is a concept that is repeated over and over throughout Disney's resorts and parks (as well as all of the company's businesses). Each resort, for example, is built around a story, and every design detail, from the landscape to the lamps, supports the theme of that story. Each park is built around multiple stories and their design, from the trash containers to the refreshments, echo those stories. From the theater language spoken to the personal appearance of cast members, the human resources of the business are an integral part of the show. Jobs are performances; uniforms are costumes. It all adds up to a seamless show.

Efficiency

The quality standard of efficiency requires the smooth operation of the theme parks and resorts. In pursuing efficiency, we provide guests with the opportunity to enjoy as much of our theme parks as they wish. Further, efficiency enhances Disney's profits, which directly correspond to the company's ability to maximize the guests' usage of the properties.

You can see this in the transport systems built for our parks and resorts. In Hong Kong, a 3.5-kilometer spur line, the Disneyland Resort Line, was added to the city's mass-transit railway system to ease the journey for our guests. At Walt Disney World, the Magical Express, a free airport-transportation service to and from the property, was created. Guests can even check their bags for their flights at their hotel and never deal with them again until they get to the baggage carousel at their destination airport. Inside the parks, buses, boats, Monorails, and Disney-designed Omnimovers keep guests moving in the most efficient manner possible.

Disney pursues operational efficiency throughout its properties. We study guest flow and usage patterns to provide the proper equipment and staffing levels. Operational checklists ensure that we are prepared for the demands of each business day. Sales levels are analyzed to provide the proper mix and quantity of products and services, establishing the optimum speed of service to ensure the best guest experience.

———⌣

It is, however, not enough to simply identify quality standards. They must also be prioritized. Otherwise, what happens when a conflict between standards arises? Consider this: What should a cast member do when a guest using a walker enters a moving loading platform that governs the speed of an entire attraction? Does the cast member slow or stop the ride and inconvenience the rest of the riders, or does she leave the guest who does not fit the mold to fend for himself?

The Disney parks and resorts have prioritized their quality standards and we have just explored them in their proper order (safety, courtesy, show, and efficiency). Once you know these priorities, the solution to the problem becomes clear. The cast member immediately knows to put the safety of a guest with disabilities ahead of the efficiency of the loading process, the continuity of the show, and even the courteous treatment of another guest. Prioritized quality standards act as the guiding signals in the pursuit of exceeding guest expectations.

Finally, like your common purpose, your organization's quality standards will surely be different from the standards at Walt Disney World. Nevertheless, they are the deliverables of the purpose, and they define and specify the criteria by which your service decisions will be made and judged.

Old Mutual Group, a South Africa–based international financial services firm, provides an excellent example. Founded in 1845, Old Mutual employs about fifty thousand people worldwide. In 2001, after a series of customer and employee surveys, the company's leaders decided to systematically improve its customer service. As Jerry van Niekerk, Executive General Manager and the champion of the new service initiative, said, "Our customers often buy a 'promise' which is delivered many years later: at the end of the term of investment or at the point of retirement. The manifestation of our commitment to deliver on these promises is found in our service."

Old Mutual's service initiative included benchmarking, which brought a group of employees to Disney who quickly grasped the power of a common purpose and quality standards. Six months later, the company adopted its own purpose: "SMILE—Service, Make It a Life Experience!" At the same time, Old Mutual adopted a set of six quality standards, summed up in the acronym "REWARD," which stands for Responsiveness, Efficiency, Warmth & Courtesy, Accountability, Reliability, and Demonstrate & Show.

By 2005, the company's efforts had paid off. Customer surveys revealed that 87 percent of the company's clients were satisfied with the company's service and, better yet, 57 percent were delighted by the service—ten points above the industry average. In addition, job satisfaction had become the top-scoring dimension in employee surveys, creating dividends in terms of employee hiring, engagement, and retention.

DELIVERING ON THE PROMISE

With guestology and quality standards to guide us, it is time to start exploring the delivery of Quality Service. At Disney, as in all organizations, there are three major service-delivery systems. These systems are the methods by which Quality Service is implemented, and they are *cast*, *setting*, and *process*.

Cast is, of course, the employees that work in your organization. If you think for a moment about organizations known for world-class service, their employees always come to mind as a key source of service delivery. *Setting* is Disney-speak for the physical and virtual resources of your organization. It is where your customers meet you. If you have ever decided to leave a restaurant before you were even seated because of how it looked or smelled, you already know how important setting is to service delivery. *Process* represents the various series of operations that are used to deliver your products and services to customers. The late W. Edwards Deming, perhaps the most famous quality guru of all, pinpointed process as the primary determinant of product quality, and it plays just as large a role as cast or setting in the delivery of Quality Service.

The next three chapters detail how these three systems are used to deliver the common purpose and quality standards at Disney, how they work in other organizations, and how they can work in your company.

Quality Service Cues

Become an expert guestologist: Guestology is the work of learning who your customers are and understanding what they expect when they come to you. Guestology techniques include surveys, listening posts, focus groups, utilization studies, and, most important, the feedback customers give to employees.

Create a guest profile: Knowledge about customers includes demographics (information about the physical characteristics of your customer base) and psychographics (information about their attitudes, lifestyles, values, and opinions). Both provide useful information for creating service quality.

Use the Guestology Compass to manage customer information: The compass collects and analyzes customer needs, wants, stereotypes, and emotions. The company can use this information at a macro level to provide mass customization, while employees can use the same tool to personalize their interactions with customers.

Articulate a unique common purpose: A common purpose defines an organization's mission, communicates a message internally, and creates an image of the organization. At Disney's parks and resorts, "We create happiness by providing the finest in entertainment for people of all ages, everywhere."

Define your critical Quality Standards: Quality standards are the criteria by which service is judged, prioritized, and measured. The four standards in Disney parks and resorts service are Safety, Courtesy, Show, and Efficiency.

Recognize the primary Service-Delivery Systems: Delivery systems are the methods by which Quality Service is implemented. Organizations have three major delivery systems: Cast, Setting, and Process.

CHAPTER 3

The Magic of Cast

It only takes a quick browse through the business section of any bookseller to see that there are countless texts devoted to the power and ability of fully engaged employees and the indispensable role they play in the achievement of organizational goals. In fact, the vital need for a fast-thinking, highly motivated workforce seems so logical and commonplace that it is hard to imagine that our beliefs about people at work were ever any different. But in the 1930s, employees did not hold as respected a place in the organizational scheme as they do today.

Even Henry Ford, who in 1914 had outraged capitalists everywhere when he nearly doubled plant employees' wages to $5 a day and in his 1922 autobiography wrote glowingly of the capacity of the American worker, had soured on the merits of the workforce by the 1930s. "The average man won't really do a day's work unless he is caught and cannot get out of it," said the inventor of the moving assembly line in a 1931 interview. He backed up this mean-spirited declaration with the force of the Ford Service Department, a group of strong-arming supervisors and security guards that, under the direction of Harry Bennett, intimidated and physically attacked Ford laborers who did not toe the company line.[1]

In stark contrast to the mechanistic gray of Henry Ford's beliefs about employees, Walt Disney's vision was awash in color and energy. As the roaring 1920s gave way to the depressing 1930s, the financial and critical success of the company's first Technicolor cartoons and Walt's dream of creating the first feature-length animated movies were driving growth at Disney's Hyperion Avenue studios in Burbank, California. Walt knew that the key to the studio's continued prosperity was its workforce. So he began an ambitious expansion plan that enlarged the six-person staff to more than 750 people, and he started thinking seriously about training and development.

If you were a young animator at Disney in 1931 and you didn't own a car, there was a good chance that several nights a week Walt himself chauffeured you and a group of your colleagues to Los Angeles for company-paid classes at the Chouinard Art Institute. In late 1932, as the attendance at these classes expanded, Walt quit driving and hired Don Graham of Chouinard to teach at the studio. "I decided to step out of their class," Walt quipped, comparing his company to the competition, "by setting up my own training school."[2] Accordingly, on November 15, 1932, the first session of the Disney Art School was held, with twenty-five students. Attendance grew quickly, particularly after word spread about the nude models Don had hired to pose in the life drawing class.

By 1934, the in-house school was running on a full-time basis. Newly hired animators were taught drawing in classes held at local zoos and learned production techniques in studio classes. Early in 1935, Walt analyzed the characteristics of a good animator to guide Don in the development of "a very systematic training course for our young animators . . . and a plan of approach for our older animators."[3] Soon, outside lecturers were appearing and Disney animators were learning from distinguished speakers, including architect Frank Lloyd Wright and drama critic Alexander Woollcott.

At the same time the company's first training programs were being established, Walt was formalizing the major elements of the corporate culture. Hard work and creativity were rewarded with bonus checks. The use of first names and casual dress contributed to an open atmosphere. Uninhibited story sessions, sometimes held after work in Walt's home, added a democratic element to a system based on adopting the very best ideas, no matter where they originated.

The first big payoff for all of the company's training and development efforts came on December 21, 1937, when *Snow White and the Seven Dwarfs* premiered in Hollywood to a standing ovation from the industry's elite. Composed of two million drawings, the critically acclaimed, eighty-three-minute feature film broke attendance records at New York's Radio City Music Hall and won a specially made Oscar that featured one regular-size statue accompanied by seven dwarf Oscars. Within six months, the receipts from the film had paid off all of the company's bank loans, and, in its first run, *Snow White* earned $8 million. This was "a phenomenal sum," wrote Disney biographer Bob Thomas, "considering that the average price for a theater admission in the United States in 1938 was twenty-three cents—and a heavy percentage of those seeing *Snow White* were children admitted for a dime."[4]

Walt made a similar investment in the training and development of people in the mid-1950s in Disneyland. In 1955, he created Disney University, the first corporate university, to make sure that new cast members understood and delivered the service he envisioned at the unique new park. And in 1971, five years after Walt's death, when Walt Disney World opened in Florida, a new branch of the University was established along with it. By then, there was no debate about the investment. Everyone knew Walt had been right when he said, "You can dream, create, design, and build the most wonderful place in the world . . . but it requires people to make the dream a reality."[5]

> *Whatever we have accomplished is due to the combined effort. The organization must be with you, or you can't get it done . . .*
> —Walt Disney

Accordingly, in the Quality Service Compass, cast members are the first critical delivery system of the common purpose and quality standards. At the Disney parks and resorts, for example, we believe that "our front line is our bottom line." The truth in this becomes clear when you consider that guests in our parks come into contact with cast more than 2.5 billion times per year.

"It might surprise you, but in our research, people cite interactions they have with our cast as the single biggest factor in their satisfaction and intent to return," said Tom Staggs, who took on the role of Chairman of Walt Disney Parks and Resorts in January 2010, in an investor call in early 2011. "What I've really come to appreciate this past year is that our cast's commitment to guest experience is holistic—from designing our parks, attractions, and resorts, to creating our entertainment offerings, and even down to the food that we serve—we want to wow our guests with every interaction."[6]

CASTING THE FIRST IMPRESSION

It has been said before and it is worth repeating: You never get a second chance to make a first impression. At Disney, all cast members know about the importance of first impressions. They understand that guests will form a first impression in seconds and how important it is to make sure that impression is a positive one. First impressions are strong and lasting ones. But customers aren't the only people who get fast and firm first impressions. So do employees.

Before we start exploring the first impressions that new cast members get at Disney, take a moment to think about what most new employees experience when they arrive for their first day of work. What was the first thing you did on your first day on the job? It was probably some kind of orientation. Almost all large organizations offer a formal new employee orientation program. It is the most common kind of training offered.[7]

Here's one more question: What is the first impression that most new employees get on that first day on the job? Those few who don't participate in an orientation program probably get a hodgepodge of impressions over which their new employers have little control. They just go to work and get to work. Those new hires who do get an orientation are mostly treated in a mechanistic fashion. They are imprinted with varying degrees of information that usually involve an official welcome, statements of the organizational mission and values, explanations of benefits and policies, paperwork processing, and, perhaps, a code of the ethics along with a menu of the penalties that code violators might expect. A few hours later, they are marching off to their new jobs, and their employers have missed a golden opportunity to begin creating a workforce capable of delivering world-class service.

Disney hires thousands of people annually. The Casting Center at Walt Disney World, for example, often handles 150 to 200 applicants each day, and as many as 100 jobs, including transfers and promotions, are filled daily. Prior to 1989, casting was conducted in an ad hoc series of offices and trailers. But in 1989, when today's center was opened, the ability to make a memorable first impression on prospective and new cast members was greatly improved.

The Walt Disney World Casting Center was designed by renowned architect Robert A. M. Stern, who immediately understood the power that the finished building would have to impress new hires. To the new cast member, the Casting Center, Stern explained, "may be the only time you experience the total identity of the corporation. It's very important symbolically." Accordingly, he created an entry point to the organization that is at once elegant and playful, one that architecture critic Beth Dunlop described as "otherworldly and fanciful, as if it had dropped from the pages of a picture book; a stop frame in an animated film."

Impression-making is an integral part of the design. As prospective cast members enter the building, they grasp door-knobs patterned after the talking doorknobs in the Disney film *Alice in Wonderland*. The receptionist's desk is on the second floor at the back of the building. As you travel toward it on your own trip down a rabbit hole, you get a symbolic tour of the company through hallways and rotundas of ever-changing shapes and perspectives. Gilded figures of cartoon characters sit atop columns, scenes from Disney animated films are painted on the walls and ceilings, and the waiting room features a model of Cinderella Castle surrounded by free-form seating. "Bob [Stern] was adamant that you enter on the ground floor, and the first time you can ask for a job is at the other end of a hall on the second floor," explained Disney project director Tim Johnson. "He said, 'Let them wander. Let them get a taste for Disney before they get there.'"[8]

Disney's casting centers aren't the only place future cast

members get their first impressions of us. Like many companies, in recent years Disney has transferred portions of its casting process to the Internet, and we use job fairs, recruitment programs, and many other methods to staff our company. But no matter what the method, we always use our brand and culture to make a good first impression and to ensure that potential cast members understand what will be expected of them as early as possible in the hiring process.

Now picture yourself walking through that wonderful, fanciful building dedicated solely to the casting process at Walt Disney World. What kind of message does the fact that the company has invested so much effort in its design and materials say about how we value our cast? How will such a company expect its cast members to behave? Now ask yourself, what kinds of messages do your employment settings and experiences send to job applicants and new hires?

OUTFITTING THE CAST FOR SERVICE DELIVERY

You might think that Walt Disney World pays a premium for extra-courteous and friendly employees or that cast members are really Audio-Animatronic figures manufactured using some secret formula cooked up by the Disney Imagineers. In fact, our cast members are hired from the same labor pool as every other organization, and they are paid the going rates. When we are successful at modeling the Disney culture and sharing the conditions of employment, we are able to hire people who are the right fit and predisposed to deliver great service. Our not-so-secret tip for providing friendly service is to first hire friendly people. Our not-so-secret method by which friendly people are then transformed into Disney cast members can be found in the way they are trained.

After a successful audition (yes, Disney-speak for a job interview) for a role, the first thing that new cast members do is begin learning how to deliver Disney's brand of Quality Service. Our parks and resorts worldwide use a multi-tiered approach to preparing the cast for service delivery:

- The first tier is a global orientation, which is conducted at Disney University and teaches concepts and behaviors that are common to every cast member throughout the organization.
- The second tier is line-of-business training that cast members require for their job category. For example, all new food-service cast members are taught food-safety procedures.
- The third tier is a local orientation that encompasses the location-specific information that is needed to perform in the different business units of the resort.
- The fourth tier is on-the-job training, which is conducted after the new cast members assume their roles.

All newly hired cast members start their tenure at Disney with Traditions, a one-day orientation program taught by Disney University, the internal training arm of the company.

At Walt Disney World, for example, the average class size is forty-five people, and there can be nine classes each week on average, with as many as fourteen classes per week in peak hiring seasons. Traditions is taught by existing cast members who serve in the role of training facilitators. Each year, a voluntary casting call is made for Traditions Assistants, a role that is considered an honor. Those cast members who are chosen leave their daily jobs at regular intervals to teach the course. (By the way, the extra depth of knowledge and refresher training acquired by the Traditions Assistants in the course of facilitating the program is an added benefit of using veteran employees to deliver training.)

The goal of Traditions was well stated by a veteran Disney Institute facilitator who said, "We don't put people in Disney. We put Disney in people."[9] Toward that end, the program utilizes a variety of training techniques, including lectures, storytelling, video, exercises, large and small group discussions, and field experiences. Traditions is designed to accomplish four major purposes:

- To acclimate new cast members to the foundations of the culture.
- To perpetuate the language and symbols, heritage and traditions, quality standards, values, and traits and behaviors of the Disney parks and resorts.
- To create a sense of excitement about working for Disney.
- To introduce new cast members to the core safety regulations.

We have already briefly mentioned the use of Traditions as the initial communicator of the common purpose and quality standards, but it does much more than that. It explains how they are put into practice in the resorts and parks. Thus, it serves as an introductory course in Disney showmanship.

Traditions, for example, explains why the cast members must have a "timeless" appearance that enables them to reflect the setting and story when they are entertaining guests. The Disney theme parks have often been complimented on, and criticized for, their strict guidelines regarding the personal appearance of cast members. While some observers have tried to politicize the issue, policies regarding hair, jewelry, cosmetics, etc. are in place for sound business reasons. They are directly and clearly related to the quality standard of Show and they are designed to ensure that we fulfill the fundamental principles of Quality Service: paying attention to the details and understanding guest expectations.

Of course, for policies like this to be legal and fair to employees, they must be consistently interpreted and applied. Disney cast members are not only informed of appearance guidelines throughout the employment process, they are informed before they even fill out an application. And without exception, no new cast member is allowed to participate in the Traditions class and thus start work until his or her personal appearance is in compliance. With all this focus and attention to detail, changes in the appearance policy are not undertaken lightly, especially since neither employees nor the legal system would look kindly on a return to a stricter policy once it has been eased. In 2000, for instance, the Disney parks amended their guidelines to allow men to wear mustaches; in 2010, it allowed women to forgo pantyhose when wearing skirts. But it made these changes only after numerous focus groups with cast members and guests determined that they did not detract from "the Disney look."

Traditions also extends our common purpose of creating happiness through entertainment into the very language that cast members speak. You have already been exposed to the show-based vocabulary used at Walt Disney World; Traditions is where cast members learn it.

Disney-Speak

Attractions: Rides, shows
Cast Member: Employee
Guest: Customer
Onstage: Guest areas
Offstage/backstage: Behind the scenes
Costume: Uniform
Audition: Interview
Role: Job
Host/Hostess: Frontline employee

At first glance, Disney's language may seem contrived or inconsequential. But words create images and corresponding assumptions in people's minds. Take the word *guest*. An unhappy guest and an unhappy consumer create two very different images in an employee's mind. Guests are welcome visitors, whom you host; consumers are statistics. If someone is your guest, don't you feel a greater obligation to ensure his or her happiness? The word *performance* also creates a singular image. If you are performing in a show, are you likely to be operating at a higher level than when you are busing tables at a restaurant? How we talk about work does make a difference.

Don't underestimate the power of a good orientation program to create a portrait of the organization and its culture in the minds of new employees. While the history, mission, and values of your business may be as familiar as a favorite childhood story to you, chances are good that your new employees have never heard them, or have heard versions of them that may not be accurate.

When St. Louis–based Dierbergs, Inc., a chain of twenty-three supermarkets employing more than five thousand people, decided to revamp its new-employee orientation process, it first studied how Disney communicates its heritage and culture. "We were doing a traditional rules-and-regulations thing," recalls Fred Martels, then Dierbergs' senior human-resources executive and now head of People Solutions Strategies, a consulting firm. "We told people what they could and couldn't do and what would get them fired. But that doesn't motivate people. We needed to speak to their hearts, not just their brains."

To accomplish that goal, the company created a new program that emphasized its 157-year history, the four generations of family management, and its heritage and culture of Quality Service. The orientation includes pictures from the company's history and stories of great customer service. Instead of spending all their time on company policy, a handbook of rules is given to employees. They are asked to read it after the class and return a signed statement agreeing to abide by the rules.

North Carolina–based Montreat College designed its first orientation program after its administrators visited Disney Institute for a program cosponsored by Washington, D.C.'s Council of Independent Colleges, a national association of more than five hundred private liberal arts institutions. Montreat College, a Presbyterian not-for-profit with three satellite campuses and about 1,500 students, appears to grow out of the mountains of western North Carolina. Founded in 1916, many of the buildings on its main campus are built from stone and timber harvested from its land, and the school's logo, a seven-stone arch featuring a keystone in the center, is patterned after one of the campus's prominent architectural features.

That logo provided the inspiration for the college's first-ever orientation program, aptly named Keystones. Like the school's logo, the new half-day program was built around seven modules: history and traditions, values, educational experience, academics, student life, courtesy, and efficiency. During the training, new employees were organized into teams of six and given a six-piece jigsaw puzzle that formed the image of a graduating student, a symbol of the ultimate goal of the school. Each kept a piece of the puzzle, and every six months they came back together for another two-hour training session that highlighted another aspect of the seven modules.

Instead of sending a trainer to Montreat's satellite schools, those staff members came to the main campus for classes. "We had a lot of people who just didn't understand our heritage," former Dean of Admissions and Financial Aid Lisa Lankford explained at the time. "They didn't understand that their jobs were an important part of the entire educational show at Montreat. Now they are starting to see."

So when new employees at Dierbergs Family Markets hit the aisles or new cast members at Walt Disney World step onto their stage or new professors at Montreat College stand in front of their first class, they all have a sense of the community they have joined. The next goal of orientation is to link that picture to specific behaviors.

THE BEHAVIORS OF QUALITY SERVICE

Over the past decades, as Disney's parks and resorts have defined and refined their four quality standards, the Traditions program has also devoted more and more time to teaching cast members how to achieve them. The class introduces all of the standards, but is particularly focused on the elements of those standards that can be applied universally throughout the organization. That means training in core safety procedures and the basic elements of courtesy.

These universal procedures and behaviors are taught using a simple role-playing exercise for judging the guest experience called "Good Show/Bad Show." A Good Show is anything leading to a positive guest experience and a Bad Show is . . . well, you've surely guessed the definition of that. The phrases "good show" and "bad show" have spread throughout the resorts. So when a cast member performs well, she is likely to get a thumbs-up from her supervisor and a hearty "Good show!" Conversely, when someone misses a service opportunity, he is likely to be asked how to improve the "bad show."

Since the first priority of Quality Service is safety, new cast members are first taught exactly how to respond if an accident should occur. Then they learn accident-prevention procedures ranging from evacuation routes to the use of fire extinguishers to emergency first-aid techniques. Even the safe use of gestures is discussed; we don't assume everyone knows to not use the tools, golf clubs, or other instruments in their hands to point out directions.

Disney University has also spent a good deal of time defining courtesy in action and exploring how courtesy contributes to a positive guest experience. The result of these efforts is embodied in a list of actions called "performance tips," which every cast member learns in the Traditions program.

Performance tips are a set of generic behaviors that ensure that cast members know how to act courteously and respect the individuality of each guest. The training addresses such topics as how to make a good first impression and offer a warm welcome. It explores the effects of posture, gestures, and facial expressions on the guest experience. And it explains how tone of voice and the use of humor can contribute to—or detract from—service delivery.

While the phrase "performance tips" may sound relatively innocuous, these tips pack a punch. At Hong Kong Disneyland and Disneyland Paris, for example, they have been translated into a set of behavioral actions called Guidelines for Guest Service. The guidelines are summarized in seven sentences and

Disney's Guidelines for Guest Service

Make Eye Contact and Smile!
- Start and end every guest contact and communication with direct eye contact and a sincere smile.

Greet and Welcome Each and Every Guest
- Extend the appropriate greeting to every guest with whom you come into contact.
    "Good morning/afternoon/evening!"
    "Welcome!"/"Have a good day!"
    "May I help you?"
- Make guests feel welcome by providing a special differentiated greeting in each area.

Seek Out Guest Contact
- It is the responsibility of every cast member to seek out guests who need help or assistance.
    Listen to guests' needs
    Answer questions
    Offer assistance (taking family photographs, for example)

Provide Immediate Service Recovery
- It is the responsibility of all cast members to attempt, to the best of their abilities, to immediately resolve a guest service failure before it becomes a guest service problem.
- Always find the answer for the guest and/or find another cast member who can help the guest.

Display Appropriate Body Language at All Times
- It is the responsibility of every cast member to display approachable body language when onstage.
    Attentive appearance
    Good posture
    Appropriate facial expression

Preserve the "Magical" Guest Experience
- Always focus on the positive, rather than the rules and regulations.
- Talking about personal or job-related problems in front of our guests is unacceptable.

Thank Each and Every Guest
- Extend every guest a sincere thank you at the conclusion of every transaction.
- Extend every guest a thank you or similar expression of appreciation as he/she leaves your area.

serve a variety of purposes. First, they define behavior in terms of the guests. They create a common baseline for interaction with guests and demonstrate the elements of performance that perpetuate courtesy, Disney-style. Second, the guidelines communicate employee responsibilities. They make the company's expectations for service delivery clear to new cast members and they provide a basis for accountability. Fulfilling the performance guidelines is an expectation. Cast members who do not use them are subject to progressive disciplinary actions.

Guest service guidelines serve yet another important purpose. They showcase ways to customize service to individual guests. Practices such as smiling, greeting, and thanking guests are all well and good, but if these actions are restricted to rote, mechanistic behaviors, their effectiveness is severely limited. They are more properly seen as minimum expectations and a guide to the creation of customized service for individual guests.

The stories of how Disney cast members tailor service based on unique circumstances of their guests are legion. For example, there is the couple with the sick child who returns to their room and finds a personalized get-well card from Mickey. It is the guest service guidelines that provide the jumping-off point for that level of service. Cast members use them to craft unique service moments for individual guests—not a bad return on seven short sentences.

Sometimes the structure of a company can present a challenge to communicating the behaviors that will support its common purpose and standards. For example, in the late

1990s, Start Holding, a temporary employment agency based in Gouda, Holland, with more than 5,100 employees in 650 storefront offices located mostly in Holland, Spain, and Germany, underscored the importance of its service quality initiative by positioning it as a leadership initiative that would ultimately cascade to all of its international and domestic operations.[10] To launch its leadership initiative, the company brought its leadership team, board of directors, and four groups of district managers to the Disney Institute and then took more than five hundred branch managers to an Institute program held at Disneyland Paris.

Start adopted a common purpose (*We create careers*) and four quality standards: Accessibility, Reliability, Service Provision, and Efficiency. But the company still needed to develop and communicate the performance behaviors that would help its widespread network of branch employees to deliver its brand of Quality Service. Start's answer was to create a system called the Service Box.

The Service Box included a series of training and motivational videotapes, issued to leaders every two months, which explained and explored another aspect of one of Start's four quality standards. Each office scheduled a training meeting for its staff coinciding with the tape's arrival. Interestingly, the videos are relatively short, less than fifteen minutes each, and are designed to serve only as a launching point for further learning. The remainder of each training session was devoted to brainstorming ideas for putting its contents to work on a day-to-day basis.

All of the ideas in the staff and operational area were then collected and communicated via what Start called Service Platforms—communication tools designed to leverage the creative effort of employees by sharing each office's solutions throughout the company.

THINK GLOBALLY, PERFORM LOCALLY

Anyone who has vacationed at the Disney resorts knows that they are a lot like huge multiplex theaters screening a variety of living, interactive movies at the same time. The movies are all entertaining. They are also all related by common production values. But each one tells a different story and utilizes a different theme. Within Walt Disney World, the Contemporary Resort has a radically different story and theme than the BoardWalk Resort. Epcot's Future World tells stories different from the 1940s Hollywood as re-created in Disney's Hollywood Studios. And so on.

The first tier of cast-delivered service training, which includes the orientation program and service guidelines, unites all cast members with common goals, language, and behavior and offers a broad outline of what is meant by Quality Service. This tier helps create the multiplex theater that is a Disney park. But to manage all the different films playing in the theater, the common purpose and quality standards must be driven down to the local level. That is done with the creation and communication of *performance cultures*.

A performance culture is a set of *location-specific* behaviors, mannerisms, terms, and values that direct and enhance a cast member's role in any particular show. Performance cultures are developed and nurtured by the management and cast at Disney's resorts and parks. Each performance culture includes its own mission, vision, and performance values (which are, of course, aligned with the larger purpose and quality standards of the business as a whole).

It might seem like a waste of time to create localized cultures in addition to an organization-wide culture, but there are some very good reasons for the practice. As we've already mentioned, the larger and more diverse the organization, the more difficult it is to create a single coherent culture that will make sense to everyone. A strong local culture speaks more directly to the day-to-day responsibilities of employees, and it strengthens the sense of ownership and involvement in the business unit. Like the performance tips, a local performance culture also can be very detailed about the behaviors that the local cast will share. And perhaps most important for the delivery of Quality Service, it establishes and reinforces the local show by tapping directly into the story and theme of the area. The result is a more memorable experience for guests.

One of the notable performance cultures at Walt Disney World can be found at the Polynesian Resort. The Polynesian was part of Walt's original vision for his new park in Florida, and, open since 1971, it is one of the property's first hotels. Most recently renovated in 2006, it is an 847-room resort set on a prime location near the Magic Kingdom. The South Seas theme and the style of the Polynesian are particularly relaxed, and it is a favorite among our guests for weddings and honeymoons.

A guest staying at the resort would surely be surprised to

learn that the Polynesian has not always enjoyed the stellar reputation it has today. In fact, in the early 1990s, an assignment to perform there was usually not greeted with much enthusiasm by cast members. The property was not scoring high marks in terms of guest satisfaction. What turned the Polynesian around? The cast, and its successful effort to create and maintain its own unique performance culture.

Under the leadership of then–General Manager Clyde Min, the cast of the Polynesian undertook the challenge by taking cues from the style and theme of the hotel itself to build a new performance culture. They studied the island cultures of the South Pacific and created new connections between traditional island values and the performance culture of the hotel. The result was a new level of service based on *hoʻokipa*, a word that describes Polynesian-style hospitality and the willingness to welcome and entertain guests with unconditional warmth and generosity.

The cast of the hotel created its own mission statement ("Our family provides a unique hospitality experience by sharing the magic of Polynesia and spirit of *aloha* with our guests and lifelong friends") and its own vision of the future. That vision called for a resort that would be a "lush tropical paradise known for creating magical lifetime memories." It also specified that the Polynesian would be a benchmark in its industry and a place where guests and cast members would be willing to sign up on waiting lists for an opportunity to visit and work.

To support the resort's new mission and vision, the cast

Disney's Polynesian Resort Values

Aloha
We love our fellow cast members and our guests unconditionally.
SAMPLE BEHAVIORS: I will take an interest in my trainees and fellow cast as individuals beyond work. I will greet and welcome every guest and cast member I meet with warmth and sincerity.

Balance
We strive for stability and vitality in our personal and professional lives.
SAMPLE BEHAVIORS: I will organize my day to accomplish everything and stick to my plan. I will assist others who need help if I finish early.

Courage
We pursue our beliefs with strength and perseverance.
SAMPLE BEHAVIORS: I will follow through with every dissatisfied guest or problem until completion. I will give honest and caring feedback and coaching to others and accept it myself.

Diversity
We seek, value, and respect differences among our fellow cast members.
SAMPLE BEHAVIORS: I will respect and learn about the diversity of my fellow cast and guests. I will translate important information for cast members who only speak my native language.

Honesty
We deal with each other in a sincere and straightforward manner.
SAMPLE BEHAVIORS: I will turn in all items found and encourage others to do the same. I will be true to myself and admit when I am wrong or need help.

Integrity
We act in a manner consistent with our words and beliefs.
SAMPLE BEHAVIORS: I will be a positive role model at all times and adhere to departmental guidelines. I will replace negativity and criticism with a positive attitude.

Kina'ole
We provide flawless guest service of our Polynesian Product.
SAMPLE BEHAVIORS: I will keep informed and updated on new information and procedures. I will do my job to the best of my ability the first time and every time consistently.

Mea ho' okipa
We welcome and entertain our guests with warmth and generosity.
SAMPLE BEHAVIORS: I will smile and start conversations with guests and cast and use their names. I will introduce my trainees to my fellow cast members and show them around the property. I will go out of my way to make each guest feel special with personal touches and interactions. I will assist and accommodate any guest need or request to make them feel at home.

'Ohana
We treat each other as a family member, supporting, encouraging, and helping.
SAMPLE BEHAVIORS: I will encourage and motivate others to make our cast and guests feel special. I will be an available resource to support my trainees and fellow cast members.

Openness
We share information freely.
SAMPLE BEHAVIORS: I will make every effort to communicate to others who speak a different language. I will give recognition to my trainees and fellow cast when a job is done well.

Respect
We treat others with care and consideration.
SAMPLE BEHAVIORS: I will respect the opinions, ideas, and feelings of others. I will pull my own weight to avoid impacting others in a negative manner. I will allow others to grow and learn from their mistakes.

adopted a series of values that furthered the themed nature of the resort by mixing traditional corporate values, such as diversity and openness, with true Polynesian values, such as 'ohana (family) and *aloha* (love and warmth). These values were then linked directly to cast behaviors.

The cast also identified and attacked barriers to guest satisfaction. Concerned that the check-in was taking too long and that guests were not arriving to an experience that welcomed them properly to the warm and rich culture of the Polynesian islands, the cast redesigned the process. Front Desk, Bell Services, and Valet cast members partnered to create a new check-in sequence that incorporated a cast-led tour of the lobby providing plenty of information about the amenities of the resort and an opportunity to ask questions. No additional costs were incurred, and the time each guest stood at the front desk was significantly reduced along with the corresponding wait for service.

The effort to revitalize the Polynesian Resort quickly bore fruit. Guest satisfaction measures improved across the board, registering increases from 21 percent to 68 percent. The number of repeat guests rose far enough to put the property in the running for a first-place finish in Walt Disney World's Guest Return rankings. Cast satisfaction ratings rose from percentiles in the 70s into the high 90s, and the resort's costs in terms of workers' compensation and safety accidents dropped until they were the lowest in Walt Disney World. Here's another statistic that speaks volumes for how cast attitudes toward the resort changed: On Bring Your Child To Work Day in 1996, only eight children visited the property; two years later, 113 children came to see where their parents worked.

Further, Disney has almost completed building another island-themed performance culture at its newest property, Aulani, a vacation resort and spa in Ko Olina on the Hawaiian island of Oahu. Imagine the power of a performance culture like that of the Polynesian Resort located in a spot where the setting and culture are indigenous to the story.

BUILDING YOUR PERFORMANCE CULTURE

Building cultures is not a science. In fact, it is a fairly mysterious process that when done well is capable of uniting the energy and emotions of the entire workforce into a laserlike focus. Anyone who has ever been exposed to such a culture can tell you that magical levels of service can be achieved. But just as often—maybe even more often—culture-building efforts fail, leaving behind high-minded statements that do not reflect any existing reality. While we can't give you a guaranteed formula for creating a performance culture, we can give you some insight into the systematic Disney approach to developing them and show you living examples of their powerful effect on business results.

If you take a closer look at the work that produced the performance culture at the Polynesian Resort and the performance culture being developed at Aulani, you will see that the implementation efforts were accomplished in three phases. First, new visions and missions are designed to align the workforce to the business unit in a more powerful way. Second, the values connected to the mission and vision are identified, articulated, and linked to behavior on the job. And finally, the workforce is turned loose to achieve the Quality Service vision it had designed.

To create a new vision and mission capable of uniting everyone working within an organization or business unit, it only makes sense that everyone, or at least a team that represents everyone, be enlisted in the effort. Employees themselves need to define their work in relation to customers and the common purpose and decide what role they will play in the accomplishment of that purpose. As an example, think about the ways in which the Polynesian's mission is similar to, and at the same time unique from, Walt Disney World's common purpose. The team also needs to consider how employees relate to each other and how they relate to customers. At the Polynesian, the cast decided to be a family, and customers became guests and lifelong friends. Finally, they need to cut the tethers that hold them to earth and dream about how their unit would look if it could become anything they wanted. This blue-sky thinking becomes the basis for a shared vision for the future.

The creation of a set of shared performance values is intimately connected to the establishment of vision and mission. Some management thinkers believe values precede mission and vision; others suggest the opposite. In either case, creating shared performance values is an important foundational element from which employee behavior and actions will follow. Identifying values should also be a team effort. The team needs

Six Tips for Culture-Building

1. **Keep it simple.** Everyone must feel comfortable with the culture. Leave room for individuality and personality.

2. **Make it global.** Everyone at the site, including management, must buy in.

3. **Make it measurable.** Create specific guidelines, and make them a part of the performance-assessment process.

4. **Provide training and coaching.** Incorporate the elements of the culture into employee training and ongoing performance coaching. Encourage peer-to-peer coaching.

5. **Solicit feedback and ideas from the team.** Foster a sense of ownership, and expand the pool of creative input by allowing employees to contribute to the show.

6. **Recognize and reward performance.** Build employee motivation through formal and informal reward and recognition programs.

to consider what values are already at work in the organization, what new values are required to support the culture, and how well they will meet the service needs of customers. As the cast of the Polynesian did, they also must consider how to link values to action by establishing behaviors that reflect the values and how those behaviors will be measured.

The final phase of building a performance culture is to give employees the freedom to begin living it. They need to consider how they will achieve their mission and vision, how their jobs impact service delivery, and how they can improve that delivery. Witness the reinvention of the check-in process at the Polynesian. Employees also need to begin the never-ending work of translating mission and strategy into action and the practicing of behaviors that reflect the performance values. Only then will the work of building a performance culture begin to produce results.

Quality Service Cues

Make a memorable first impression: First impressions are lasting ones. Start sending the right messages to prospective and new employees from the very first point of contact.

Communicate the heart and soul of the organization first: Your heritage, values, common purpose, and quality standards are more important than the paperwork associated with new hires. Use new-employee orientation sessions to communicate your organizational vision and culture.

Speak a service language; wear a service wardrobe: How you look and how you speak communicates an image in the customer's mind. Make sure that your appearance and language reflect your brand of Quality Service.

Establish a set of basic performance guidelines: The guidelines are a set of behaviors that ensure that employees know how to act courteously and respect the individuality of each guest. They form the baseline for delivering and measuring Quality Service performance.

Build a performance culture: Performance cultures are sets of location-specific behaviors, mannerisms, terms, and values that direct and enhance an employee's role in a specific business unit. They use shared values, visions, and missions to help the workforce optimize and customize service delivery.

CHAPTER 4

The Magic of Setting

W alt Disney was an Oscar magnet. He was personally nominated for Academy Awards on sixty-four occasions, the most nominations ever recorded. He won thirty-two Academy Awards, also the most ever. After a couple of dozen trips to the dais, picking up Oscars probably began to feel a little routine to Walt, but the first, which he accepted in 1932, must surely have been a thrill. That year, Walt received the first award ever presented in the new category of Best Cartoon for *Flowers and Trees*, the twenty-ninth film in the *Silly Symphony* series and the first ever made using a new color process called Technicolor.

The innovative use of color in a cartoon was the main reason that *Flowers and Trees* was such a sensation among both audiences and critics, but it is notable for another reason. The short film showcased the possibilities of setting like no other cartoon ever had before. In it, two young trees fall in love, but their happiness is threatened by a jealous rival—in this case, a gnarled stump. The old stump sets the forest afire to separate the lovers, but is itself consumed. The forest returns to life, and the young lovers are wed. The woodland setting and the music, by Mendelssohn and Schubert, communicate the story to the audience. In fact, the setting, which in other cartoons of that era would have only provided the background for the action, had suddenly become the entire film.

In 1938, Walt and the Disney Studios picked up two more Academy Awards. This time, one of the studio's inventions, the multiplane camera, received an award in the Scientific and Technical category, and the first film made with the camera, another *Silly Symphony* entitled *The Old Mill*, won for Best Cartoon. The multiplane camera represented another major step in capturing the full potential of setting. It allowed Disney animators to overcome what Walt's biographer Bob Thomas called "the essential flatness of the animated film."[1] The camera could be pointed and moved through stacks of animation cels and glass plates, creating the same effect as a live-action camera moving through a set. The result was a depth of setting that had never been seen before. The multiplane camera created a fantasy world that was more convincing because audiences saw it in the same way that they saw life. "When we do fantasy, we must not lose sight of reality," explained Walt.[2]

In 1940, when *Fantasia* was released, Walt's innovative use of setting was again much in evidence. Broomsticks marched and flowers and mushrooms danced. *Fantasia* also broke new ground in the use of sound, an important element of setting. The film used Fantasound, which recorded music using several microphones and played it back through a corresponding number of speakers. Walt received another Academy Award for this technical breakthrough. Unfortunately, the outbreak of World War II closed down *Fantasia*'s foreign markets, and the expensive audio equipment needed to properly present the film made domestic theater owners reluctant to show it. *Fantasia* cost $2.2 million to make, more than four times the cost of the average live-action film at that time, and it flopped on first release. Two decades later, in the 1960s, it was rereleased, took a new generation of moviegoers by storm, and was proclaimed a classic of animation.[3]

Walt's insistence that animated films must be believable to the audience to be effective was translated directly into the settings of Disneyland. You might think that Walt's idea for the first theme park was met with instant acclaim, but that was not the case. In the late 1940s, as Walt became more and more intrigued with creating his own kind of amusement park, he got less and less support for the idea. Walt's brother Roy, his longtime business partner and the holder of the company's purse strings, did not see the financial merit in this risky leap beyond their current business and was reluctant to fund the idea. In 1952, Walt got tired of waiting and, with his typical drive, went ahead without the rest of the company. He created a new corporation, WED Enterprises, Inc., and funded it by borrowing against his insurance policies and selling his vacation home in Palm Springs. He also hijacked the first class of

Imagineers out of the Disney animation studios, stashing them in empty offices and workshops around the property to work on the park.

Since the people who designed and built Disneyland came from the animation side of the business, they treated its settings as integral and important parts of the park from the very first. Disneyland was going to be a living movie that its guests would experience by moving through it. And, as in animated films, to make that vision come to life, the audience had to have the opportunity to become totally immersed in the experience. "Disneyland is a show," said Walt, and every detail of the setting had to support the show.[4]

> *Disneyland is like Alice stepping through the Looking Glass; to step through the portals of Disneyland will be like entering another world.*
> —Walt Disney

"Walt was asked why he worked so hard to make it all look realistic," recalls Imagineer Tony Baxter. "He said what we're selling is a belief in fantasy and storytelling, and if the background wasn't believable, people wouldn't buy it."[5] With the benefit of 20/20 hindsight, the soundness of Walt's thinking is obvious. The audience didn't simply buy the idea of Disneyland; they fell in love with it.

The role of setting in the Disney theme parks was revitalized in the mid-1980s when Michael Eisner assumed leadership of The Walt Disney Company. Michael didn't know much about theme park construction, but he knew how to create compelling entertainment.

"He was a movie guy—ABC, Paramount," explained Peter Rummell, who headed up Disney's construction projects worldwide at the time. "For months, every time he saw PUD [planned unit development] on a plan, I'm convinced he thought it meant 'producers using drugs.' But what he did bring was a total understanding of what Disney is; what its strength is; what it represents to the world. You all know the horribly overused real estate maxim 'location, location, location' as a key to success. Michael's chant very quickly became 'entertainment, entertainment, entertainment.' He was consistent and unrelenting."[6]

Two weeks into his new job, Michael suggested building a hotel shaped like Mickey Mouse. It wasn't feasible, but to Disney insiders, the freshly hired CEO's willingness to swing for the fences signaled a whole new ballgame in terms of setting. Shortly thereafter, Michael scrapped plans for two new, but architecturally mundane, hotels at Walt Disney World. It was a gutsy move that risked a long-term relationship with a valued development partner, but it paid off. The 1,514-room Walt Disney Dolphin Hotel and the 758-room Walt Disney Swan Hotel replaced the canceled hotels. Designed by world-renowned architect Michael Graves, they created a new standard for setting in the Disney resorts.

The Swan and Dolphin signaled a renaissance in Disney

architecture. Soon, the best architects in the world were working on commissions for the company. At Walt Disney World, resorts such as the Grand Floridian, Wilderness Lodge, Board-Walk, and Yacht Club and Beach Club (the latter designed by Robert A. M. Stern) took setting to a whole new level. "Our hotels became experiences and entertainments in themselves," wrote Michael in his book *Work In Progress.* "Successful as our hotels are in artistic terms, the simplest tribute to them comes from our guests. To this day, the occupancy rate at each of them runs in excess of ninety percent—the highest in the world."[7]

Setting continues to play an essential role in the delivery of Quality Service throughout Disney. As you watch Disney films, board its ships, shop in its stores, and visit its parks, look closely at the details of the environment you've entered. You will find a surprising level of depth and coherence. Think about how this enhances your experience.

SETTING DELIVERS SERVICE

If you ask most businesspeople how their company delivers service to customers, they will surely mention people and processes (the topics of the last and next chapters respectively) as the primary delivery systems. But the idea that an organization's setting can deliver service is less well understood. Can a setting really deliver anything at all? And if so, how does it deliver service?

In fact, setting can deliver both the physical and psychological aspects of service. At the Disney theme parks, for example, there are many attractions where cast members will load and unload guests, but the bulk of the service experience is delivered during the ride by the setting itself. This is becoming more and more common in all businesses. In these days of e-commerce, we are witnessing a transformational shift in physical service delivery from employees to setting. When you buy books, music, or any one of what seems like a zillion other products and services available online, you are served by a setting—that is, the Web site from which you are buying. In most of these transactions, you are the only human involved in the sale. The setting and electronic processes are delivering service. Employees are involved in the creation and maintenance of the setting and, after the fact, in the fulfillment of orders.

The use of setting to deliver the psychological aspects of service is similarly common. All organizations, knowingly or unknowingly, build messages to their customers into the settings in which they operate. Picture a luxury car dealership and a used car lot. Now, a theme park and a carnival. And now, a designer clothing retailer and an outlet store. In each pair, consumers are buying similar products—cars, entertainment, and apparel. But in each case, the setting in which they buy these products is communicating a great deal about the quality of the products and the level of service they can expect, not to mention the effect it has on the price they are willing to pay.

As noted in Chapter 1, the simple fact is *everything* speaks to customers. Not only does everything, animate and inanimate, speak, it also acts upon customers. The messages delivered by setting establish and change customer perceptions about the products and services that we sell. As R. Buckminster Fuller, one of most original thinkers and inventors of the twentieth century and the creator of the geodesic dome on which the 180-foot-tall Spaceship Earth in Epcot is based, aptly said, "You can't change people. But if you change the environment that the people are in, they will change."[8]

In short, setting is *the environment in which service is delivered to customers, all of the objects within that environment, and the procedures used to enhance and maintain the service environment and objects.* It is a critical point on the Quality Service Compass, and it is vital that settings be designed and managed to effectively communicate and deliver service to customers.

In Disney-speak, setting is the *stage* on which business is conducted. At the Disney resorts, the primary setting is known as "inside the berm." The phrase originated at Disneyland, where Walt had a low landscaped hill, a berm, constructed around the property to physically delineate its boundaries. The berm blocked out external distractions, such as highways and buildings, which might interrupt the living movie he was building. "I don't want the public to see the world they live in while they're in the park," said Walt. "I want them to feel they're in another world."[9] The sharp contrast between the world on the outside of the hill bordering Disneyland and the one inside the hill prompted cast members to start identifying being at work as being inside the berm.

It only takes a short tour of any of the Disney resorts to see how seriously every detail is managed inside the berm. Further, the idea of managing the setting inside the berm is not restricted to physical properties. The Disney Web sites that describe and promote our resorts are part of the setting, as are the telephone systems used to take reservations and communicate with guests and the Disney gift kiosk in the Orlando airport. Elaborately themed Monorails and motor coaches are part of the setting and communicate service messages to guests, too. Any setting in which our guests come into contact with us must deliver Quality Service.

Selected Components of Setting

Architectural design
Landscaping
Lighting
Color
Signage
Directional design on carpet
Texture of floor surface
Focal points and directional signs
Internal/external detail
Music/ambient noise
Smell
Touch/tactile experiences
Taste

As the definition above states, setting also includes the objects within the environment. At the Disney resorts and parks, that means the furniture in the hotel rooms, the utensils in the restaurants, the trees and flowers on the property, and, of course, the attractions in the parks. All these objects contribute to the delivery of entertainment to guests. If the bed is uncomfortable, the silverware clunky, the plants sparse, and the rides jerky, who would want to return for a second visit? With an ever-increasing number of choices available for spending their shrinking leisure time and hard-earned money, how many instances of poorly designed setting would it take to drive a guest away forever? These are increasingly important questions to which today's successful organizations must continually find answers.

Finally, setting includes the work of maintaining and enhancing the environment and the objects within it. Even the best-designed setting must be continuously maintained and improved. Attractions must be kept in good repair, rooms must be cleaned, plants fed and watered, etc. A poorly maintained setting is just as telling as a poorly designed one.

If it all sounds like a lot of work, that's because it is. Creating practical magic is hard work, and it is a tenuous business that is entirely dependent on attention to detail. Listen to how the late and legendary Imagineer John Hench described it:

> Interestingly enough, for all of its success, the Disney theme show is quite a fragile thing. It just takes one contradiction, one out-of-place stimulus to negate a particular moment's experience . . . tack up a felt-tip brown-paper-bag sign that says "Keep Out" . . . take a host's costume away and put him in blue jeans and a tank top . . . replace that Gay Nineties

melody with rock numbers . . . place a touch of artificial turf here . . . add a surly employee there . . . it really doesn't take much to upset it all.

What's our success formula? It's attention to infinite detail, the little things, the little, minor, picky points that others just don't want to take the time, money, or effort to do. As far as our Disney organization is concerned, it's the only way we've ever done it . . . it's been our success formula. We'll probably be explaining this to outsiders at the end of our next two decades in the business.[10]

One organization that does not need further explanation about setting is Metairie, Louisiana–based East Jefferson General Hospital. East Jefferson, a not-for-profit hospital with more than 450 beds, began its own Quality Service journey at the Disney Institute and went on to implement a wide variety of improvements in its setting.

Committed to a common purpose that states, "Providing care and comfort is our highest mission," the hospital undertook a series of design changes in everything from the landscaping of its grounds to a new design for its Intensive Care Unit (ICU). Staff began parking in a neighboring parking lot and taking a shuttle to work so that patients and visitors could use the parking lot on the hospital's grounds. When a new parking garage was erected, it was designed so guests would not have to walk more than thirty-five steps before encountering a staff member.

East Jefferson's ICU was transformed into a model of service delivered through setting. For this twenty-bed critical-care area, East Jefferson created two rows of ten rooms lining a wide corridor. Almost the entire front wall of each room was glass, curtained for privacy, that could be swung open like a door, allowing X-ray and other bulky equipment to be moved near the patient. An X-ray development station was installed in the unit so images could be processed and read on the spot.

The ICU's interior room walls were lined with shuttered bins and cabinets. Everything a critical-care nurse needed was within a step or two. So that nurses could stay in constant contact with patients, the traditional nurses' station was redesigned into a series of counters featuring telephones and computers that were located just on the other side of the glass walls of the patients' rooms. Patients and on-duty nurses are almost always within eyesight of each other. The patient care and efficiency of operation built into East Jefferson's ICU setting won the ICU Design Award jointly given by the Association of Health-care Architects, the Foundation of Critical Care Medicine, and American Association of Critical Care Nurses.

IMAGINATION + ENGINEERING = IMAGINEERING

It is impossible to discuss the role of setting at Disney without taking a few minutes to talk about Walt Disney Imagineering. The word *Imagineering* was coined by Walt himself. When asked about Disney's success, he replied, "There's really no secret about our approach. We keep moving forward—opening new doors and doing new things—because we are curious.

And curiosity keeps leading us down new paths. We're always exploring and experimenting . . . we call it Imagineering—the blending of creative imagination and technical know-how."[11]

Imagineering is The Walt Disney Company's master planning, creative development, design, engineering, production, project management, and research and development arm. Representing more than 150 disciplines, its talented corps of more than 1,600 employees is responsible for the creation of Disney resorts, theme parks and attractions, hotels, water parks, real-estate developments, regional entertainment venues, cruise ships, and new-media-technology projects. Its motto: *If you can dream it, you can do it.*

When you marvel at the attractions in the Disney theme parks, with their detailing and special effects, you are paying tribute to the Imagineers' work. They are the people who first imagine and then design and build our settings. The Imagineers have produced some of the world's most distinctive experiential storytelling, including using Audio-Animatronics characters to tell the swashbuckling tales of Pirates of the Caribbean; developing a faster-than-gravity "freefall" through another dimension in The Twilight Zone Tower of Terror; and integrating high-speed, large-format film projection with a breakthrough ride system to take guests on a breathtaking hang glider flight in Soarin' Over California. In the process of developing its unique projects, Walt Disney Imagineering has been granted more than 115 patents in areas including ride systems, special effects, interactive technology, live entertainment, fiber optics, and advanced audio systems.

How do Imagineers create settings that deliver Disney's common purpose and quality standards? Former Imagineer Vice Chairman Marty Sklar gave a concise answer to that complex question when he created a list of setting-design principles he labeled Mickey's Ten Commandments. "They came out of the Imagineering process and what I've learned from my principal mentors, Walt Disney and John Hench," Marty explained. They set the stage for the rest of this chapter.

1. *Know your audience:* Before creating a setting, obtain a firm understanding of who will be using it.
2. *Wear your guest's shoes:* That is, never forget the human factor. Evaluate your setting from the customer's perspective by experiencing it as a customer.
3. *Organize the flow of people and ideas:* Think of setting as a story, and tell that story in a sequenced, organized way. Build the same order and logic into the design of customer movement.
4. *Create a "wienie":* Borrowed from the slang of the silent-film business, a wienie was what Walt Disney called a visual magnet. Such a magnet is a visual landmark that orients and attracts customers.
5. *Communicate with visual literacy:* Language is not always composed of words. Use the common languages of color, shape, and form to communicate through setting.
6. *Avoid overload—create turn-ons:* Do not bombard customers with data. Let them choose the information they want when they want it.

7. *Tell one story at a time:* Mixing multiple stories in a single setting is confusing. Create one setting for each big idea.

8. *Avoid contradictions; maintain identity:* Every detail and every setting should support and further your organizational identity and mission.

9. *For every ounce of treatment, provide a ton of treat:* Give your customers the highest value by building an interactive setting that gives them the opportunity to exercise all of their senses.

10. *Keep it up:* Never get complacent, and always maintain your setting.

With the Imagineer's Commandments in mind, let's take a look at two major uses of setting: its ability to send messages to customers and its use as a guide to the service experience.

SENDING A MESSAGE WITH SETTING

As guests move from one attraction to another at Disney parks, they are told new stories. These stories, or themes, change from attraction to attraction and from park to park. They extend into the hotels and restaurants. Setting plays a primary role in the delivery of each of those stories. When setting supports and furthers the story being told, it is sending the right message.

One of many examples of this can be seen at the entrance to the Magic Kingdom at Walt Disney World. When you arrive at the main gate, you scan your pass and enter the park through the turnstiles. You are now in an outdoor lobby that features phones and restrooms. Once past the lobby, you walk into one of two short tunnels leading into Main Street's Town Square. The tunnels are lined with posters "advertising" the attractions within. As you leave the tunnels, even first thing in the morning, you smell fresh popcorn, which is made in carts placed near the tunnel openings. The experience of entering the park is explicitly designed to remind guests of the experience of entering a movie theater. There is the ticketing, the turnstiles, the lobby, the halls to the screening room lined with posters displaying the coming attractions, and even the popcorn.

As stories change, so must their setting. The Disney parks are noted for the beauty of their landscaping, but no one who enters the Haunted Mansion would call it well manicured. At Walt Disney World, as guests line up to enter the ride, they find themselves under a canopy that cuts off the bright Florida sunlight before it reaches earth. They pass an abandoned cemetery in which the leaves lie where they have fallen from the trees and the plants are wild and stunted from the lack of light. Inside the mansion, dust and cobwebs are everywhere. This level of dishevelment is tough to maintain. The park purchases dust in five-pound bags and sprays it over the attraction with a kind of reverse vacuum cleaner. The cobwebs are made from a liquid that is strung up by a secret process.[12]

The resorts of Walt Disney World also make good use of setting messages. The Wilderness Lodge is located right next to the Contemporary Resort, but the modern world never imposes on the Lodge's American West setting. Guests can't see the Contemporary; the views are purposely blocked. They enter the lodge along a winding road that is flanked by tall pine trees and dotted with old-fashioned streetlights and a BEAR CROSSING sign. If you walk straight through the main lobby and out of the building, you see a long view over a completely undeveloped lake that is meant to remind guests of the open spaces and natural wonders of the U.S. National Parks. Lest you get the impression Disney can control everything, notice the Spanish moss hanging from the pines on the property. It doesn't grow out West, but no matter how hard the landscaping team tried, they couldn't get it to stop growing in Florida. They bowed before Mother Nature.

Disney isn't the only organization that tells stories. Every organization tells its own unique stories to its customers, and those stories must be supported and furthered by setting. For example, New York City–based professional services powerhouse PricewaterhouseCoopers (PwC) sends a compelling message to prospective employees by borrowing Walt Disney World's setting. One of the Big Four accounting, auditing, and consulting firms, with more than $26.6 billion in annual revenues, PwC employs 160,000 people globally, and like many large companies, it uses an internship program to attract the best and brightest college students to its doors. A significant portion of PwC's interns get job offers upon graduation, and that's why PwC brought the setting of Walt Disney World, along with Disney Institute training, into the picture.

In 1998, and for years afterward, PwC concluded its annual internship program by bringing its entire class of interns to Walt Disney World for five days of training and fun that they called *Discover the Magic.* An instant hit with students, the program sent a compelling message about how much PwC values their potential. "The trip seemed to cap off what would be an exciting internship from start to finish," said Kevin Post, an intern from Lehigh University. "The idea of traveling to Florida at the end demonstrated an enormous commitment. It was apparent that PwC recognized that their greatest asset was the individual."[13]

In 2011, PwC relaunched the program. This time, the company decided to boost the job offer acceptance rate of graduating interns by inviting the 2,400 of them who had been offered full-time jobs to Walt Disney World. The curriculum includes professional insights, learning, leadership training skills, and personal enrichment sessions. Its goal, according to Paula Loop, PwC's U.S. and Global Talent Leader, is "a high energy, unforgettable experience that helps prepare interns for their full-time career."

Another organization that counts students among its customers is Dover, Delaware's Wesley College, a 2,500-student private school affiliated with the United Methodist Church. After attending a Council of Independent Colleges seminar at the Disney Institute, Wesley administrators decided to take better advantage of their setting during the open houses held to introduce prospective students and their families to Delaware's oldest private college (founded in 1873). "We needed to help the admissions staff do more than point to a building and say, 'That's the science building,'" explained then–Acting Vice President for Academic Affairs Lorena Stone. "We needed to tell a memorable story during our campus tours."

The newly designed open house tour was not much longer than the old one, but it included a new path and scripts designed, as Dr. Stone said, "to bring the college to life for students." For instance, the new tour started in the amphitheater, where the college's graduation ceremonies take place and prospective students are shown where they could be four years later. At the Cannon Building, where the science classes are held, the admissions guides told the story of Annie J. Cannon, a noted female astronomer who taught at the school and invented an identification system for stars still in use today. And at the Campus Community School, which offers educational programs for local children, the teachers-to-be in the audience got a good look at the field experience they would gain without leaving the campus. At Wesley, the setting helped to sell the college to prospective students.

A good exercise to better understand the messages delivered by the setting is to visualize a store that you patronize or, better yet, actually visit it. Drive up to the front entrance and look at the signage and landscaping. What impression do they convey about the business within? Enter the business. Look at the entryway. Is it clear how to proceed? Is the store clean and orderly? What does the store itself tell you about this company? Continue to observe the setting throughout the process of making a purchase. At each step, think about what the setting is telling you. Now, return to your own organization. Approach it like one of your customers and repeat the exercise. What does your setting tell customers?

Sometimes, looking through a customer's eyes takes an adjustment in perspective. Disney's Imagineers have been known to don knee pads and crawl around the parks to experience them from a child's perspective. The next time you walk down Main Street in the Magic Kingdom, notice how low to the ground the windows of the shops extend. They allow children to see the displays as comfortably as adults can.

As John Hench declared, telling a story through setting means getting the details right. An organization can't send customers a believable message regarding Quality Service unless every detail of setting supports it. An overflowing trash basket or a dead plant can undercut a message about the quality of your product or how much you care about your customers in a single glance. A sign with missing letters or misspelled words tells customers something about your company. A Web site with dead links or a page that won't load properly communicates a negative message. When you are telling a story to your customers, make sure that your setting is sending messages that reinforce your story.

GUIDING THE GUEST EXPERIENCE

Setting can do much more than simply create an impression in a customer's mind and reinforce the story you are telling. It can also be used to assist customers as they proceed through the service experience. Cues in the setting can orient customers, explaining where they have been and where they are going. They signal changes and provide direction. When the components of setting are used to instruct customers, we say they are guiding the guest experience.

Anyone who has been to the Magic Kingdom already knows that Disney's theme parks are laid out around a central hub. This design came directly from Disneyland, where Walt Disney first used it to guide guests.

"This is the hub of Disneyland, where you can enter the four realms," explained Walt to his future biographer Bob Thomas during a preopening tour of the park in 1955. "Parents can sit in the shade here if they want while their kids go off to one of the other places. I planned it so each place was right off the hub. You know, when you go to a world's fair, you walk and walk until your feet are sore. I know mine always are. I don't want sore feet here. They make people tired and irritable. I want 'em to leave here happy. They'll be able to cover the whole place and not travel more 'n a couple of miles."[14]

Walt's hub design does more than ease tired feet. It also directs guests. In the Magic Kingdom at Walt Disney World, for example, there is one entrance to the park, which leads guests onto Main Street, U.S.A. From Main Street, there is only one direction to go—forward toward the hub, which offers direct access to each of the park's lands and serves as the central return point for movement throughout the park. Behind and looming over the hub is a beacon, Cinderella Castle, the most visible feature inside the park. The castle draws guests up Main Street and into the heart of the park. As Mickey's Ten Commandments specify, it is the wienie, the most important of all the visual magnets in the Magic Kingdom.

Guests can also move between the lands in the Magic Kingdom, and when they make those transitions, they experience another concept borrowed from the world of film: the cross-dissolve. A cross-dissolve is used to get the movie audience from one scene to the next. The Disney Imagineers explain how it works in the parks as follows:

> A stroll from Main Street to Adventureland is a relatively short distance, but one experiences an enormous change in theme and story. For the transition to be a smooth one, there is a gradual blending of themed foliage, color, sound, music, and architecture. Even the soles of your feet feel a change in the paving that explicitly tells you something new is on the horizon. Smell may also factor into a dimensional cross-dissolve. In a warm summer breeze, you may catch a whiff of sweet tropical flora and exotic spices as you enter Adventureland. Once all these changes are experienced, the cross-dissolve transition is complete.[15]

The spaces between two distinct areas and other peripheral areas in your place of business, such as parking lots and waiting rooms, are especially important places in which to use setting for service delivery. Customers usually have low expectations of these in-between areas, and small investments in effort can yield exceptional impressions.

The central hub and cross-dissolve are two major examples of how setting guides guests at the Disney parks, but there are many more setting cues that direct guests. Landscaping is an important signaler of direction, and signage is an obvious guide. Color can also give directional cues. For instance, ice cream wagons in our parks are often blue, signaling a cool refreshment. Popcorn wagons are red, signaling a warm treat.

The University of Chicago Hospitals & Health System (UCH) is a 451-bed medical complex located on Chicago's South Side that is consistently ranked among the nation's top hospitals by *U.S. News & World Report*. As a Disney Institute client, UCH considered every detail of its service experience and expanded its definition of setting well beyond its property boundaries to ensure that its setting was doing as good a job guiding its patients as its expert staff was.

"We flowcharted the home-to-home experience—even with details like what signs were on the expressway and what kind of support materials were provided in advance," explained Jeff Finesilver, who was Vice President and Director of UCH's Center for Advanced Medicines at the time. "We also created a valet parking experience—the Center for Advanced Medicine now operates the busiest valet parking experience in the entire city of Chicago. We also paid attention to architectural features, from skybridge signage to elevator and hall signage—all the onstage and backstage areas—to maintain decor and facilitate a smooth experience for visitors."

The use of setting as a tool for guidance is not confined to physical space. It works in the virtual world as well. We have all had the experience of being shuffled through a voicemail labyrinth only to reach a dead end that leaves no alternative but to hang up and start over again. When customers call your organization, how well does the phone system guide them to their desired destination? Web sites can be even more annoying. Every online shopper has had the experience of filling an electronic shopping cart full of goods only to have it dumped off a cyber cliff on the way to checkout. Is your site designed to be intuitive for customers? Does it cut customers off in the middle of their transactions? Setting needs to be managed wherever your customers meet you.

APPEALING TO ALL FIVE SENSES

Taking full advantage of setting in order to enhance the customer experience means designing for all five senses. People understand their environment and gather impressions through sight, sound, smell, touch, and taste. Each sense offers an opportunity to support and enhance the show created for guests.

Sight

About 70 percent of the body's sense receptors are located in our eyes, making sight the greatest transmitter of setting. Obviously, as we've already noted in our examples, the Disney parks are designed to display delightful and entertaining views wherever guests look. Sight lines are a major consideration. What you see and, just as important, what you *don't* see from your hotel window or from anywhere else on the properties is carefully planned.

Color is considered throughout the parks. For instance, many guests comment on the unusual purple-and-red color scheme on the directional signs on the public roads in and around Walt Disney World. As an experiment, flags of different colors were once set out on the property and guests were asked which ones they remembered seeing. Purple and red were the colors they recalled most often.

The Imagineers are experts in the uses of color and have created their own "color vocabulary" that defines how certain colors and patterns act on guests. "Different projects call for different uses of color," explained Nina Rae Vaughn, the former Director of Concept Design & Illustration at Walt Disney Imagineering. "If a project wants to communicate 'fun,' as in [Disneyland's] Mickey's Toontown, I will experiment with bright colors, applying the brightest of brights against the darkest of darks. If the idea says 'adventure,' like the Indiana Jones Adventure, I will use colors that shout action and excitement. These are hot reds and oranges, with shades of complementary colors like blues, that make the hot colors even more vibrant."[16]

Sound

Sounds are caused by vibrations of infinitely varying pitch, quality, and loudness. In designing setting, the only vibrations guests hear should be good ones. If you have ever found yourself unable to banish from your mind the tune from a Disney attraction, such as "It's a Small World," you know the power of sound in setting. As John Hench said, "People don't walk out of attractions whistling the architecture."[17]

To get an idea of how sophisticated the sound systems get at the Disney parks, listen to the parades on Main Street. At Walt Disney World, a single cast member working a mixing board controls the audio portion of the parades. Speakers on the floats are synchronized with 175 speakers along the parade route so that no matter where you are viewing the parade, you are surrounded by an appropriate audio track. How does the sound track move in tandem with the parade? There are thirty-three sound zones along the parade route, and sensors are embedded in Main Street. As each float triggers a sensor, the sound track for that float "moves" along with it.

Guests aren't the only people who respond to sound—cast members do, too. When Hong Kong Disneyland installed "CostuMagic," an RFID-based self-serve system that cast members use to obtain their costumes, sound played an integral role. As they check out each garment using scanners in kiosks, a sound like a bubble popping tells the cast member that it has been successfully scanned. When checkout is complete, Tinker Bell's "magical jingle" plays, signaling a completed transaction. "We wanted our cast members to feel the magic when checking out their garments," explained costume manager Soon Kuan Yeap. If there is problem with checkout, such as an incorrect garment or size, a buzzer notifies both the cast member and the department's costume assistants that help is needed.

Smell

There are approximately five million receptor cells in the human nose, and it is only a short trip from there to the brain. Smells are stored in our long-term memory. In fact, scientists have found that if you associate a list of words with smells, you will better remember the words.

At the Disney parks, smells are used to help deliver magical memories. We've already mentioned the popcorn carts positioned at the entrance tunnels to the Magic Kingdom. Vendors don't sell much popcorn at 8:30 in the morning, but the corn is already popping. The smell of popcorn communicates the "living movie" message of the park. A little farther on, the bakery on Main Street purposely pumps the scent of fresh baked goods into the street to support the story of America's small towns.

Touch

The skin is the largest organ in the human body, and touch is the sense that resides there. Whether it comes through the hands or feet or face, people get lots of data from the tactile properties of our environment and the objects within it. At the Disney parks, the sense of touch is considered in the walkways, attractions, hotels and restaurants, and everywhere else.

The touch of water is an integral part of many of our attractions. At Walt Disney World, water splashes on guests to heighten the experience at Catastrophe Canyon during the Disney's Hollywood Studios Backlot Tour and in Jim Henson's

Muppet∗Vision 3D show. The water parks and resort pools are all about touch. Young guests love the surprise fountains all around the property. They spend hours trying to anticipate from where and when the next stream of water will shoot.

Touch, or the lack of it, is also the sense that we play to when the elevator in The Twilight Zone Tower of Terror drops underfoot and plunges thirteen stories. To intensify the experience, the Imagineers created a ride that drops even faster than the speed of a free fall.

Taste

There are about ten thousand taste buds in the human mouth, and each taste bud contains roughly fifty taste cells that communicate data to our brains. Walt Disney World's eateries cater to as many of those cells as possible with a wide range of dining experiences.

In addition to hundreds of restaurants featuring a vast selection of food at our parks and resorts, menus change as the setting dictates. From turkey legs in Frontierland to saltwater taffy at Disney's BoardWalk, tastes follow setting as well as the preferences of our guests. World Showcase at Epcot in Walt Disney World is a 1.3-mile tour of global cuisine; it is just a few short steps from the sushi in Japan to the freshly made fettuccine in Italy.

Sight, sound, smell, taste, and touch—designing and delivering Quality Service means appealing to all of your customer's five senses.

ONSTAGE AND BACKSTAGE

Another major consideration in the delivery of quality customer experiences through setting is the separation of onstage and backstage activities. In Chapter 1, when we introduced the concept of practical magic, we talked about the distinction between being onstage and backstage at our parks and resorts. "Onstage" is all public areas of the park, where guests roam freely and service is delivered. "Backstage" is all of the behind-the-scenes areas where guests don't go, a place where all the mechanisms and technologies that run the property (and all the people that run them) reside and where cast members can move freely and prepare themselves to go onstage. Both are part of the overall setting.

The first and best reason to keep onstage and backstage areas separated is that anything that does not support or enhance the Quality Service experience detracts from it. Just as important as what we see, hear, smell, touch, and taste is what we *don't* see, hear, smell, touch, and taste. For example, no hotel guest needs to see the laundry or the power plant. Restaurant-goers find stacks of dirty dishes an unappetizing sight. Guests should not hear cast members sharing private conversations, etc.

Second, it is an unnecessary expense to design and maintain backstage areas to the same standards as onstage areas. In fact, expensive lighting fixtures and elaborate moldings don't stand much of a chance of surviving unscathed in corridors where mechanized carts and forklifts are moving supplies.

Finally, the presence of customers would be a distraction to employees at work behind the scenes. An electrician repairing a faulty circuit breaker doesn't have attention to spare for a guest. Equally important, employees need somewhere that they can relax—it is difficult to be onstage all day. Giving cast members a real break is important. You won't see or hear Disney movies and music playing in the employee cafeterias and break areas in our parks and resorts. The cast members come to those places to eat and unwind; they are not working.

At the Magic Kingdom in Walt Disney World, the separation of onstage and backstage required some careful planning. Built on wetlands, where the water table is on or very close to the surface of the ground, the park did not have the luxury of basements. Instead, the land had to be raised so that the ground floor of the site could be used for utility purposes. The public area of the parks was built on top of it, on the second floor. The ground-floor backstage area is called the Utilidor (shorthand for "utility corridor"). It covers more than nine acres and includes 1.5 miles of corridors.

Utilidors are workspaces and so are clean, practical, and composed of materials and painted in colors that you won't see onstage, such as cinder blocks that are painted institutional grays and greens. Unlike the pathways above, they run in straight lines designed to get cast members to their destinations as quickly as possible. Using the Utilidor under the Magic Kingdom, for example, cast members can don their costumes and get anywhere in the park in just a few minutes. That way there is no need to ever worry about a pirate popping up in Tomorrowland.

The Utilidors are connected to other backstage areas "above" the ground. These areas are often located only a few feet from the onstage areas, but thanks to the use of visual screens, guests never see them. On Main Street, for example, the side streets often end in a suitably decorated gate or doorway with a polite sign that signifies a cast-only area. On the other side of that door is an environment that looks more like the back of a supermarket or a manufacturing plant than a theme park. The view from inside the park is blocked by the design of the set itself. If a building needs a second story to screen the view, it is built.

The Wolfsburg, Germany–based Volkswagen Group, which borrowed its setting from Walt Disney World's to create a memorable dealer launch for the New Beetle, built the onstage/backstage distinction into its Volkswagen Marketplace concept, then the ideal design for its dealerships worldwide. One feature of the Marketplace plan was the construction of backstage areas for the sales staff. This is a place where they can get offstage, take a break, or have meals. It doubles as a meeting and training area.

"Salespeople need a place where they can let their hair down without appearing rude to the customers, so we moved these functions behind the scenes," explained Bill Gelgota, now the Southern Region Marketing Manager of Volkswagen of America. "We want to control our environment like Disney does. The worldwide design standard helps us control and reinforce the experience we think the customer wants to have."

With all of Disney's emphasis on the separation of the onstage and backstage areas of setting, it was slightly ironic to discover that guests wanted to visit backstage. It turns out that they are intensely curious about how the stories in Disney's parks and resorts are brought to life. In response to repeated requests for a look behind the curtain, we created a number of behind-the-scenes tours that are, of course, as carefully scripted as the onstage entertainments. If your customers are curious to see how your products and services are created, a well-crafted behind-the-scenes look may be just the ticket to improve their service experience.

The Volkswagen Group also accommodated its customers' desire for a behind-the-scenes look at their dealerships. The company understood that although purchasing a new car takes an hour or two, car owners often spend much more time than that in the service department over the life of their vehicle. As a result, customers want to be assured that the service component of their purchase, delivered in the back of the dealership, is as pleasant as the sales component delivered in the front.

The carmaker built that assurance into the setting of its ideal dealership. One of the important design elements of VW Marketplace was the opening of the sales floor onto the service department. In this way, new buyers were able to see the service areas of the dealership, get a feel for where they will spend time during service visits, and see the product—the new cars—being prepped for delivery. The sales process, by the way, was redesigned to take advantage of this seamless connection between sales and service. When customers bought cars, they were given a tour of the service area and introduced to the dealer's service advisers.

Before we leave this topic, it is important to note that organizations or departments that aren't directly customer-facing also have an onstage and backstage component. Their "back door" is always someone's "front door," whether that someone is a supplier or a fellow employee or a job applicant. Thus, the setting in these situations should be well-maintained and communicate what is happening onstage in the organization. As some social scientists have theorized the "broken window" theory suggests, if backstage areas are allowed to deteriorate, chances are good that the neglect will spread to onstage areas.

MAINTAINING THE SETTING

Most of this chapter has been devoted to describing elements and principles of setting that are usually addressed during the design and construction phases. But there is one more important subject to discuss before moving on: the maintenance of setting. Once you have created the perfect setting, the work of keeping it that way begins and continues as long as the setting is in use. Maintenance means more than just keeping the setting clean. It also means protecting it from damage and repairing wear and tear.

After onstage and backstage field experiences, our Institute facilitators often ask program guests to estimate the size of the maintenance cast at the Disney parks and resorts. The replies vary widely, but the correct answer is always a surprise. There are close to 120,000 people maintaining the setting at Disney's parks and resorts. That is because maintenance is an integral part of every cast member's role. From Bob Iger on through the ranks, you will never see a cast member pass by a piece of trash on the property or ignore a physical detail of the parks needing repair.

Keeping our parks and resorts clean is part of our organizational culture. It's a habit that can be traced directly back to Walt himself. "When I started on Disneyland," he once recalled, "my wife used to say, 'But why do you want to build an amusement park? They're so dirty.' I told her that was just the point—mine wouldn't be."[18]

There is also, of course, a large dedicated maintenance staff at all of our resorts. They work around the clock keeping the settings pristine. Streets are cleaned daily; the restrooms every thirty minutes. There are horses on Main Street, but you have to be on the spot to see any of their natural byproducts; the costumed custodial cast is never far behind. Maintenance technicians are on hand to make sure that all of the attractions run smoothly during the day. The staff swells into the hundreds after the parks close and the scheduled maintenance and repairs are made.

Maintenance is a significant expense in any large organization and so should be designed into the setting whenever possible. When journalist Scott Kirsner visited backstage at the Magic Kingdom in World Disney World, he was struck by the technology employed to maintain the landscape.

Based on input from the weather stations, MaxiCom's PC-based software determines how much water each of the property's 600 zones needs. Each has up to 10 individually watered beds; when a message comes in from the gardeners that a row of azaleas at [Disney's Hollywood Studios] is drying out, the horticulturist will increase the amount of water delivered there each night. When a torrential rainstorm passes over the property, the MaxiCom system adjusts by watering less—about 50 automated rain cans that measure by hundredths of an inch are scattered around the property and plugged into the network. "Every morning at 1:25, we download the data to cluster control units (CCUs) situated around the property," says [horticulture manager Scott] Shultz. The CCUs manage the sprinkler timers, which govern 50,000 sprinkler heads between them. Shultz's crew also prowls the property daily in a van equipped with a laptop and cellular modem, troubleshooting the whole system—one of the most sophisticated large-scale irrigation setups anywhere.[19]

The same level of sophistication is used throughout our parks. Hong Kong Disneyland installed a state-of-the art system to irrigate its 18,000 trees and one million shrubs. After the park closes at night, a computer directs hundreds of sprinklers, which deliver the exact amount of water, calculated by the needs of each individual plant and the weather, across the 618-acre park. This system achieves a 40 to 45 percent water saving compared to traditional irrigation systems and a 70 percent reduction in use of fresh water compared with similar theme parks.[20]

In the watering of the landscape and throughout our properties, the cast and maintenance technology combine to create a continuous and consistent focus on keeping the setting in perfect repair. As a result, the setting supports and enhances the guest experience and delivers Quality Service.

Quality Service Cues

Define your setting. Setting is the environment in which service is delivered to customers, all of the objects within that environment, and the procedures used to enhance and maintain the service environment and objects.

Tell your story through the setting. Walk through the service experience in your organization wearing the customer's shoes. Observe and critique the setting, and align its messages with the service story you want to tell.

Guide the customer experience with setting. Consider the directional aspects of setting. Make sure the physical layout of your organization (or Web site or phone system), interior design, and signage keep customers on the track for a great service experience.

Communicate Quality Service to all five senses. Customers build their impressions of you using all of their senses. Ensure that your customers' experiences with the sights, sounds, smells, touches, and tastes of your organization are consistent with expectations and with your theme.

sight
sound
smell
touch

taste

Separate onstage and backstage. Screen business functions that do not involve customers so that they do not interrupt the delivery of service. Give employees a backstage space to rest and relax.

Maintain your setting with a consistent, comprehensive effort. Use the design process to build maintenance into the setting, and enlist every employee in the maintenance effort.

CHAPTER 5

The Magic of Process

A kid in a garage. It is the starting place of many a contemporary business legend. Apple Computer, Amazon.com, and Cisco Systems were all started in their founders' home garages. Walt Disney was once a kid in a garage, too.

In 1920, at the age of eighteen, Walt got his first taste of animation at the Kansas City Film Ad Company. He was drawing figures that were used in advertising films seen in local movie theaters. In what would become a personal trademark, Walt felt constrained by the primitive technology used on the job, and he pushed himself and the company's head, A. Vern Cauger, to improve the quality of the company's minute-long ads. He even convinced Cauger to lend him a stop-action camera, which he brought home to a "studio" that he and his brother Roy had hastily constructed in the family garage.

The result of the loan was three hundred feet of cartooning that satirized the poor road conditions in Kansas City, which Walt sold for thirty cents a foot to the Newman Theater Company. Audiences liked his cartoon so much that he was engaged to produce one each week. The Newman Laugh-O-gram was born, and soon after, Walt founded a new company to make them, Laugh-O-grams Film, Inc. This company would not survive very long, but Walt had become an animator.[1]

Alone at night, working in the garage, Walt probably did not think much about process. In those first animations, the images were drawn, cut out, and pinned to a background in poses meant to simulate motion, then photographed. The resulting film was crude, with flat, one-dimensional characters. Sound and color were, of course, still years away. Walt simply decided on a subject and strung together enough drawings to create the number of feet of film needed. But if you had asked the young animator to articulate his methods, he would have described processes—the mental process of telling the film's story and the physical process of making the film itself. Walt was using process to deliver entertainment.

By the 1930s, the role of process in the creation of Disney animation was much more explicit. In the fast expansion following the success of Mickey Mouse, Walt could no longer remember every detail of every cartoon in production or take a hand in every creative decision. He needed to formalize an approach to the daily operations of the company, so he began to construct the processes that would manufacture and deliver the Disney brand of entertainment.

THE MAGIC OF PROCESS

> *People still think of me as a cartoonist,*
> *but the only thing I lift a pen or pencil for these*
> *days is to sign a contract, a check, or an autograph.*
> —Walt Disney

Previously, Walt and artist Ub Iwerks would huddle in an office and create the continuity script and drawings for a cartoon. They would emerge with a complete work and hand it over to the staff to be animated and produced. Now the cartoons were scripted and drawn using a team-based creative process in which no one person dominated. A flexible Production Unit was assembled in which a director oversaw the entire project, a stylist created the mood and atmosphere, a storyman told the tale, and a story sketchman drew the first rough visuals. The characters were developed—their voices and bodies created and refined. A sort of crude movie was made, a story reel combining the story sketches and sound tracks, before the work on the finished film began. Throughout this preliminary process, the team, Walt, and others outside the team would examine and think and argue and contribute ideas. And that was just the beginning—huge chunks of work, such as the layout, animation, sound track, and filming, were still to come.

The Disney process did not tame animation. Like any creative endeavor, it remained chaotic and, according to insiders, ever-changing. "In spite of constant efforts and persistent claims, Walt never did build an organization in the strictest sense of that word. What he built was a loosely unified group of talented people with particular abilities who could work together in continually changing patterns. They did this with a minimum of command and a maximum of dedication. What Walt wanted was the greatest creative effort—not the most efficient operation," wrote Frank Thomas and Ollie Johnston, two of the Nine Old Men, as the Disney animating supervisors during that golden era of animation were known.[2] The interesting thing is that their description sounds exactly like the structures that so many companies are trying to create today. Walt had built a flexible organization around a process-based structure.

To simultaneously organize work and, instead of stifling energy and creativity, to actually enhance it, is an accomplishment that is rarely achieved. To accomplish it in a niche business like animation was even more unusual. That's one reason why biographer Richard Schickel wrote, "That any young man was willing to attempt such a business must remain as a permanent tribute to his stubbornness. That Walt Disney, alone of all the men who went into animation, was able to emerge from it a full-fledged tycoon (several made a bit money out of it eventually) must stand as a tribute to organizational abilities of a very high order."[3]

When it was time to design Disneyland, Walt brought the same process orientation he had applied in the studio out into the physical world. There was one important difference now. To make an animated film, you ran it through the process once and created a finished product that could be viewed over and over without additional work. In a theme park, each process had to run continuously and turn out the same outcomes each time. (Theme parks are, in fact, an odd kind of process industry. Instead of producing petroleum or chemicals, their output is entertainment.) Walt knew that the key to delivering Quality Service in a living movie meant designing defect-free processes and flawlessly repeating them.

There was one big advantage to working with repetitive processes that were delivering a standardized product versus making a single product, like an animated film. And Walt realized it immediately. He told a reporter:

> The park means a lot to me. It's something that will never be finished, something I can keep developing, keep "plussing" and adding to. It's alive. It will be a live, breathing thing that will need changes. When you wrap up a picture and turn it over to Technicolor, you're through. *Snow White* is a dead issue with me. I just finished a live-action picture, wrapped it up a few weeks ago. It's gone. I can't touch it. There are things in it I don't like, but I can't do anything about it. I want something live, something that would grow. The park is that. Not only can I add things, but even the trees will keep growing. The thing will get more beautiful year after year. And it will get better as I find out what the public likes. I can't do that with a picture; it's finished and unchangeable before I find out whether the public likes it or not.[4]

Walt could fine-tune Disneyland's processes to his heart's content, and he did. He called this effort at continuous improvement "plussing," and he applied it everywhere in the park. He would wear old clothes and a straw farmer's hat and tour the park incognito. Dick Nunis, who was at the time a supervisor in Frontierland, remembers being tracked down by Walt during one of these visits. Walt had ridden the Jungle Boat attraction and had timed the cruise. The boat's operator had rushed the ride, which had ended in four and a half minutes instead of the full seven minutes it should have taken.

"How would you like to go to a movie and have the theater remove a reel in the middle of the picture?" demanded Walt. "Do you realize how much those hippos cost? I want people to see them, not be rushed through a ride by some guy who's bored with his work."

Dick and Walt took the ride together and discussed the proper timing. The boat pilots used stopwatches to learn the perfect speed. Weeks went by until one day Walt returned. He rode the Jungle Boats four times with different pilots. In the end, he said nothing, just gave Dick a "Good show!" thumbs-up and continued on his way.[5]

Plussing is still an important part of the Disney culture. If something can be made better, it's done. Disneyland Paris was originally named Euro Disney, but to Europeans, the resort's target audience, the word *Euro* signified currency and commerce. This did not create a picture of the Happiest Place on Earth in most of our guests' minds, so the name was "plussed."

When the Disney Store retail chain was first getting off the ground in late 1980s, then-CEO Michael Eisner starting visiting newly opened locations on weekends á la Walt. He studied the details, weeding out substandard products and analyzing the lighting, presentation, and service experience from the guest's perspective. The late Frank G. Wells, then Disney's President and COO, insisted that the stores adopt service standards and offer Traditions-like employee training. The two executives knew that building a successful retail chain required a standardized process that lived up to the Disney name and could be transplanted to every new store. And as Michael said at the time, "If the boss cares, I had long since learned, then everyone else cares." The process-building and plussing efforts paid off. By 1991, there were 125 stores generating more than $300 million in revenues.[6] By 2010, there were more than 350 Disney Stores with annual revenues approaching $1 billion.

PROCESS AND COMBUSTION

Processes, in their broadest meaning, are a series of actions, changes, or functions that are strung together to produce a result. They combine human (cast) and physical (setting) resources in various ways to produce different outcomes. A car is produced using a process that combines parts and labor in specific sequences on an assembly line. An appendectomy is performed using a process that combines medical staff and an operating room in a sequence of actions. All organizations can be thought of as a collection of processes.

A process delivers a result. That is, it delivers an output, such as a product or service. In fact, more than three-quarters of service delivery in most industries and institutions is process-based. And since Quality Service is all about delivery, it is critical to pay special attention to processes.

On the Quality Service Compass, *processes* are composed

of the policies, tasks, and procedures that are used to deliver service. Think of process as a railroad engine. If the engine does not run properly, it does not matter how friendly the conductor acts or how attractive the passenger cars look, the train will still not move and the passengers will not pay their fares. Process is the engine of Quality Service.

We can take the engine analogy one step further and talk about the workings of the engine. Engines are driven by combustion. A diesel or gasoline engine is powered by internal combustion. The fuel is fired inside the engine; it explodes and moves the pistons. In a steam engine, the combustion takes place outside the engine in a boiler that creates pressurized steam that in turn moves the pistons. Service processes are more like a steam engine. The combustion is externally produced—by guests. It derives from their satisfaction and repeat business and recommendations. For the purposes of Quality Service, guest-produced combustion is the best kind. When guests are powering the engine, we know that the process is focused properly on their needs.

When service processes work smoothly, their key combustion points are controlled. Quality Service is delivered without a hiccup and everyone wins. However, when combustion points are out of control, service processes misfire. Guests are inconvenienced, and unless their problems are solved, combustion points can easily turn into explosions. Identifying and controlling combustion points are an important part of delivering service through process.

The best way to identify key combustion points is to study

your customers. What do they complain about? Where do they get stuck during the service experience? What are the common problems they face when interacting with your organization? The answers to these questions are *combustion statements*. Combustion statements are important clues to the process issues you need to address in order to deliver magical service.

Let's examine some common hassles about which guests complain:

- **"This is taking too long!"** Anyone who has ever spent too much time on hold with customer service or waited too long for food at a quick-service restaurant knows this lament. What does it indicate? It tells us that we have a problem with the flow of the service experience that needs to be solved.
- **"No one knows the answer!"** We've all been faced with guests who have been bounced from place to place in search of an answer to a question. When you hear this, it means that the communication process between cast and guest has broken down.
- **"My situation is different!"** Creating a standardized process is a great way to serve the typical guest, but what about the guest who has special wants or needs? When you hear this it means the process itself is not able to accommodate certain guests.
- **"I'm stuck in a dilemma!"** Finally, processes are not infallible, and sometimes they just don't work as planned. When you hear this it means that there is a problem

with a service process that needs to be diagnosed and repaired. The more complex the dilemma, the more rigorous the problem-solving needs to be, perhaps including guestology research and the assistance of specialized cast members, such as industrial engineers.

These combustion statements are not uncommon at the Disney parks and resorts. You have probably heard them from your customers, too. That's because these examples relate to four service-process issues that are universal: customer flow, employee-to-customer communication, customers with special needs, and poor process design. These are typical combustion points in service processes, and in the remainder of this chapter, we will take a closer look at how to keep them from becoming explosion points.

GUEST FLOW

"These lines are too long!" Our guests hate long lines. In fact, long lines are the most frequent customer criticism heard in the theme park industry. On Disneyland's opening day, a day that Walt Disney afterward labeled "Black Sunday," the guest flow was a fiasco. Counterfeit tickets turned what had been planned as an invitation-only event into a mob scene as an estimated 33,000 guests overwhelmed the park. Every street within ten miles of the front gate was jammed with traffic. One of the first questions Walt addressed after Black Sunday was how to better manage those lines.[7]

THE MAGIC OF PROCESS

Overly long lines are a service-process issue that involves the flow of the guest experience. If you run a Web site, the flow of service can be impeded by slow-loading pages or over-loaded servers that can't handle a rush of customer activity. If you operate a manufacturing company, the production flow might be blocked by a certain assembly task or a parts shortage or an inefficient machine. No matter what the specific service or product being delivered, wait time is the enemy we are all fighting.

Solutions to the wait-time conundrum tend to fall into three separate categories. To minimize wait time, we can optimize the operation of the product or service process, the flow of guests themselves, or the experience of being on the line itself. At the Disney resorts and parks, all three solutions have been implemented.

- *Optimizing the operation of product and service processes* means managing your assets in ways that minimize waits. Consider giving guests access to your facilities earlier or later than usual. You can also cut wait time by extending access on a selective basis, such as opening some services prior to others or opening key areas earlier than the rest of the organization. Another idea is to provide special access to your best guests. In this way, you can reward loyalty and reduce wait times simultaneously.

  One program designed to optimize the operations at Walt Disney World is called Extra Magic Hours. Every day, one of the four theme parks opens an hour early and closes up to three hours later than usual for those guests staying at resorts on the Disney property. This provides a group of valuable customers the chance to experience the parks when they are relatively uncrowded, and the program pays additional dividends by helping to reduce the number of guests enjoying the parks at peak hours. The Rope Drop program is another example of optimizing the operation. Here, selected services, dining areas, and retail stores open prior to the opening of the rest of the park. Guests get early access and can eat, shop, and otherwise prepare for the day and be ready for their favorite attractions as they open.

- *Optimizing guest flow* means enabling guests to self-manage their movement through the service experience. These techniques are designed to give guests the gift of time. They provide choices about how guests will spend their time and provide those choices up front, before guests get caught in a wait. They also include educating guests about the benefits of certain choices and monitoring flow continually so you can offer them accurate information with which to make their decisions.

    At Disney, guests can begin to learn about their options long before they arrive at the entrances to the parks themselves. The best-selling Birnbaum's guidebooks to the parks offer suggestions for getting the most value from Disney vacations. The brochures and guides provided at the parks also include plenty of tips for making the most of a visit.

Another feature you will find at a central location in the Disney parks is the Tip Board. An idea developed by the cast, the Tip Board lists the major attractions within the park and estimates the current wait at each. Updated regularly, Tip Boards allow guests to plan their travels within the parks and minimize the time they spend standing in lines. (Wait times on the Tip Boards are slightly overestimated, because a shorter-than-expected wait is much preferable to a longer-than-expected one.) Greeters also play an important role in helping guests manage their visits. These cast members are dedicated information sources whose role is to guide guests among the many entertainment choices in the parks.

- *Optimizing the queue experience* means managing otherwise unavoidable wait time in a service process to maximize the guest experience and minimize their discomfort. We can accomplish this feat by testing products and services to be sure wait times are minimized before opening them to the public. It is also important to clearly explain wait times at the start of a process and, as mentioned above, do your best to stay under the maximum time quoted. You can instruct and prepare guests to move through a process efficiently and, during waits, use the opportunity to educate, inform, and entertain them. You can also measure the lengths of the waits and make sure your cast members understand their impact on guests.

Like the parks' Tip Boards, each attraction has its own wait-time posting that guests can see before they step into the line. And we make sure to build the theme and entertainment into the queues themselves. The cast members are trained to entertain and otherwise occupy the attention of guests waiting in line, and the setting is designed to make waits seem shorter. For instance, as guests wait to enter Jim Henson's Muppet∗Vision 3D show at Disney's Hollywood Studios, they are entertained by a twelve-minute preshow. Muppet characters move across a bank of television monitors and drop hints about the show to come.

In the past few years, the Imagineers have taken the queue experience a step further by creating interactive queues. For instance, the graveyard that guests pass on their way into The Haunted Mansion has been expanded, and elaborate crypts with interactive features have been installed. When guests reach the tomb of the composer, for example, they find instruments carved into it. Touch it and music begins to play. At Soarin', the queue includes giant video screens with motion detectors and heat sensors; groups of guests can play video games on them as they wait to enter the attraction. Why make such an investment? "Guests were willing to wait 12 percent longer because of the interactive experience," explained Walt Disney resorts and parks Vice President of Research Lori Georganna.[8]

Finally, Disney's resorts and parks business makes liberal use of several techniques designed to test and reduce wait times before we open attractions to the general public. At the Disney parks, for example, Cast Preview Days introduce the cast to new attractions and help to ferret out process flaws before guests arrive. Recently, a shipload of lucky cast members took a preview cruise on the *Disney Dream* to ensure that it was guest-ready. They were asked to have fun, but also to evaluate the entire service experience, including wait times. Guests are invited to attend Sneak Peeks, pilot tests in which a limited number of guests get an advance look at new attractions, which offers us an opportunity to further refine our service processes before the grand opening.

Perhaps the most effective weapon in the war against wait time is Disney's FASTPASS Service. First introduced in 1999, FASTPASS is an innovative computerized reservation system. When guests arrive at a FASTPASS attraction, they can choose the traditional wait in line or swipe their admission pass in a turnstile, which in turn produces a pass good for a one-hour usage period. The guests simply return during the specified hour and are processed through a shorter, dedicated line directly into the preshow or boarding area of the attraction. FASTPASS almost eliminates the infamous theme park lines. It also allows park guests to visit less crowded areas, shop, or stop for a bite to eat while waiting for their ride, instead of standing in line.

St. Simon's Island, Georgia–based Rich SeaPak Corporation is a Disney Institute client that worked hard to remove wait

---

Factors Affecting Guest
Perceptions of Wait Time

Disney Institute client University of Chicago Hospitals (UCH) surveyed patients about expectations regarding patient wait times. Although some wait time is a reality, most UCH patients in the study commented less on the length of the wait than how the wait was handled. Three important dimensions relating to patient care are:

- **Access**—Patients want access to care and are frustrated by voice mail, scheduling difficulties, and restrictions.
- **Respect**—Patients describe a strong need to be recognized and treated with dignity.
- **Information communication**—Patients express fear that they are not being completely informed.

---

time from its order-management process. A subsidiary of the largest family-owned frozen foods manufacturer in the United States, Rich Products Corporation, Rich SeaPak is a leading producer of frozen seafood and snack products and the leading retail brand within the frozen specialty shrimp category. The company enjoys a broad customer base that includes grocery stores, wholesale clubs, restaurant chains, and food-service clients, and it processes tens of thousands of orders annually.

Over the years, however, SeaPak's order process had grown unwieldy. Customer orders moved between several information systems that were developed at different times. SeaPak associates had to move between systems to locate orders and there were "stop–and-gos" where orders paused in the process.

The company knew that if it reengineered the process, it could improve its service delivery and increase profits.

A cross-functional team of twenty-five SeaPak associates, who visited the Disney Institute to study Quality Service and creativity, rethought how orders are managed from the customer's initial contact through fulfillment, billing, and the payment of invoices. They created a less complex, integrated information system capable of eliminating pauses by processing orders in a continuous flow, providing instant order-information access to customers at any point in the process and eliminating errors in the billing process. The new order process will cut days off SeaPak's order flow. It also solves a common problem among food-products companies by tracking inventory and pricing variations in real time, with the goal of producing perfect invoices every time.

Creating the perfect open-house process was the goal of a fifteen-member team at North Carolina's Lees-McRae College, a six-hundred-student, 110-year-old private institution known for its performing arts program. After attending the Disney Institute, the college decided that the open-house programs it holds each year for prospective students and their families needed some sprucing up. "There was nothing actually wrong with the way we had been conducting open houses," former Vice President for Enrollment and Student Development Alan Coheley explained. "They were nice and helpful, but they weren't providing a 'wow,' a memorable experience for our guests."

To build some wows into the program, the open-house team decided to expand their view of the process and considered the entire guest experience, from the arrival of an invitation to visit the college until the completion of the program itself. They then used storyboards, a technique discussed in the next chapter, to rework the open houses in three phases.

First, the team refined the preparation phase of a guest visit by redesigning elements such as the directions to and descriptions of the area and the program that guests receive in the mail. Second, they improved the arrival phase and started welcoming guests before they set foot on campus through the use of techniques such as sending a representative from the college to meet and greet families as they checked into the local hotel. Finally, the team reengineered the entire on-campus portion of the experience by adding a county-fair theme to their open houses. As guests moved from location to location around the campus, they found a new attraction in each spot. These attractions informed and entertained guests at the same time. Even the menus for the programs were adjusted to reflect the kinds of foods you might find at a fair. The new open-house process extended the college's control over its guest experience, it built some fun into the college search process for prospective students, and, not least of all, it ensured that when it came time to make their final choices, Lees-McRae stood out in the minds of students and their parents.

CAST-TO-GUEST COMMUNICATIONS

"When does the three o'clock parade start?" This is a very common guest query in the Magic Kingdom. It is so frequently asked that Disney University uses it as an example in the Traditions program; the Disney Institute uses it as well. The guests who ask this question are not dumb; they know the parade starts at three o'clock. What they are really asking is what time the parade will get to a certain location or where the best place to see it is or what its route is. In fact, the only wrong answers to the question are "Three o'clock" or a wisecrack.

Answering guest questions is a regular task in all organizations. How well and how efficiently these questions are fielded has an oversized effect on how guests rate the service experience. Is there any person on the planet who likes getting an answer that makes them feel stupid? Or likes being bounced from place to place in search of an answer to what should be a simple question? The only varying factor is exactly how long people will hang on before losing their cool altogether. When that happens, combustion becomes explosion.

On properties the size of Disney's resorts and parks, with annual guest lists of tens of millions of people, effective guest communication is a critical element in service delivery, and much of that communication flows directly from the cast to the guests. Accordingly, Disney's performance tips require cast members to seek out guest contact, to listen to and answer questions, and to always offer assistance. But it is not enough to simply tell the cast to help guests; they must have the information they need to fulfill that task. Thus, we have a wide variety of service processes aimed at preparing our cast to give guests the answers they need on the spot. These processes are designed to provide the right information in the right manner at the right time. Some of them are meant to disseminate information to the cast throughout Disney's properties. At Walt Disney World, for example, there is a biweekly newspaper written by and for the cast, *Eyes & Ears*, which has a bigger circulation than many community newspapers. It includes articles about new projects, attractions, and events, executive messages, etc. Pocket-size fast-facts cards have been printed and distributed so that cast members have information about new attractions and special events at their fingertips. And, of course, the corporate intranet has become an ever-more-effective means of communication over the past decade.

Creating awareness among our cast members about all the attractions and resources in the resorts and parks is an important process. When Disney's All-Star Movies Resort, catering to value-oriented guests, was preparing to open in Walt Disney World, the resort held an "Open Mouse" and invited all cast members, their families, and friends. In addition to refreshments and character appearances, the resort staff made sure their fellow cast members learned about the new hotel by creating an on-site tour contest. Each internal guest received a map of the site that was stamped at locations along the tour route. They turned the maps in at the end as entries in prize drawings.

Job-shadowing techniques are also used to teach cast members about other areas of the properties. When the catering and convention services team at Walt Disney World's Coronado Springs Resort wanted to spread the word, they planned Convention Mousenap, during which high-performing cast members from around Walt Disney World were "mouse-napped" and spent a day learning about the resort's amenities and capabilities. Internal trade shows are also held periodically and give cast members a chance to share their best practices throughout the organization. And there is a central repository for information at the Walt Disney World Library and Research Center, whose archives include thousands of Disney-related publications, news clippings, and press releases as well as statistical information for the exclusive use of our cast.

There also are techniques designed to communicate site-specific information to the cast members who perform in each area of our parks and resorts. They help avoid information overload by communicating detailed information to each specific site's cast members, but not to the larger population. Some of the site-specific techniques we have used over the years are simply scaled-down versions of property-wide techniques. There was a biweekly newspaper, *Bus Bulletin*, for bus-transportation cast members. The cast of the retail stores were given Merchantainment Cue Cards, a collectible card series, similar to the fast-facts cards, which featured a Disney character on one side and character trivia along with policy and procedures on the other.

Other site-specific communication techniques are designed for the separate performance cultures. For instance, cast members get up-to-the-minute information by attending preshift meetings that are known around the property as "homerooms." After finding that cast members who started work between shifts were sometimes missing important information, the cast of The Land Pavilion attraction in Epcot took the homeroom concept a step further. They started videotaping the daily meeting and created a backstage area where all employees could watch it before they started their daily performance.

Speaking of backstage areas, it is almost impossible to walk through any of them without seeing the ubiquitous bulletin board. Backstage Communication Boards convey loads of information on changes in policy and procedures, recent improvements, anticipated guest counts, and overall business performance. Similarly, for last-minute news flashes, Electronic Message Display Boards are positioned so cast members will see the news before walking onstage.

One thing worth noticing is that few of Disney's processes for enhancing cast-to-guest communication are complex. This is not a coincidence. The important point is not how sophisticated your communication methods are but how well and how thoroughly they prepare your staff to assist customers. In fact, the less time and money spent on communication the better—it is, after all, an overhead cost. Concentrate instead on providing critical content and memorable presentations in the simplest ways possible.

Of course, sometimes the simplest communication method is also a high-tech solution. Witness Houston, Texas–based Crown Castle International Corporation (CCIC). Beginning with its founding in 1994, CCIC raced to a leading role in the wireless communications industry with an aggressive series of acquisitions. By the end of 2010, this Disney Institute client owned or leased almost 24,000 wireless tower sites—71 percent of those in the U.S. in the hundred largest wireless markets in the United States. One of the leading providers of wireless infrastructure, CCIC leases to cellular telephone service providers, television and radio broadcasters, and other customers needing wireless networks.

As CCIC grew in the late 1990s, it expanded its vision far beyond leasing space on their towers to the delivery of world-class turnkey wireless services. CCIC customers could choose to contract for a complete network or any portion thereof. This breadth of service, the international nature of the business, and the rapid addition of acquired assets added up to a unique cast-to-guest communication conundrum. CCIC had to assist its technical personnel in the consistent and reliable delivery of the full range of complex service offerings no matter where they were located.

After discovering that each of its customers had a different definition of what turnkey service meant, CCIC began mapping every detail of every product and service process it delivers. In essence, it created process modules that its engineers could combine to build a customized solution for each customer.

"By taking all the processes necessary and breaking them down into definable areas and steps, we formalized our approach to service delivery across the company," explained the company's former COO John Kelly. The process modules guided employees through the design and implementation of the service package and ensured high quality and fast delivery. And LiveLink, a feature on the CCIC corporate intranet, delivered all of that knowledge directly to its engineers. Thus, the information that CCIC's cast needed to serve their guests was delivered where and when they needed it.

SERVICE ATTENTION

Have you ever gotten lost in a voice-mail system that offers a litany of options that don't fit your particular need, with no instructions for connecting to a live person? How did you respond? Perhaps you picked a choice at random or blindly punched the phone's operator or star keys hoping to transfer to a human being. Maybe you just hung up. How did you feel about that service experience? When you get stuck in an unresponsive phone system, you are traversing a service process that simply does not work for you. It might work for the vast majority of people who can use it, but that isn't much consolation to those of us who can't.

This is why it is so important to acknowledge and, when possible, incorporate the individual needs and desires of guests in service delivery. It is also another way in which we achieve the second quality standard in the Disney resort and parks: the standard of courtesy. Toward that goal, there is a genre of processes that serve guests whose needs cannot be satisfied by existing processes that we call *service attention processes.*

There are two key ingredients in creating effective service attention processes. First, there must be appropriate resources to make the guest experience a good one. Second, the availability of those resources must be communicated to cast and guests. Here is a closer look at how the Disney parks and resorts extend service attention to three groups of guests who don't always fit the standard profile: international visitors, small children, and guests with disabilities.

International Guests

Today's global organizations often serve an extraordinarily diverse customer base. At Walt Disney World, for example, roughly 25 percent of guests live outside the United States, and while all guests come to Walt Disney World to be entertained, international guests bring along a whole range of different expectations, behavioral habits, and needs. For instance, non-English-speaking guests will have trouble reading signs, to say nothing of understanding cast members and other guests.

If you visit Walt Disney World in the summer, you will often see large groups of Brazilian children, inseparable and clad in brightly colored T-shirts. Brazilians tend not to want ice in their drinks, and since gratuities are usually included on the bill in Brazil, they also tend not to tip. In Brazil, people like to tour in large groups and stay close together, often singing and chanting. As you might imagine, when a crowd of happy, boisterous children singing in Portuguese converges on a queue, it can be a disconcerting experience for other guests and cast members who are culturally predisposed to want more personal space.

To better serve Brazilian guests, Portuguese-speaking cast

members are on hand to support their visits and to act as translators. There are brochures and guides in Portuguese for guest use. Cast members learn about Brazilian culture and behavior. And finally, Walt Disney World works with Brazilian tour guides to break down cultural barriers and maximize their guests' experiences. The service attention focused on Brazilian guests has been well worth the effort. Their attendance quickly grew until Brazilians were among Walt Disney World's top three most frequent foreign visitors.

Small Children

Even though kids of all ages love the Disney parks, the parks are not always designed to fit the needs of our smallest guests. Some attractions pack in too much excitement for small children; others might bore them. Small children also have different concerns and needs than adult guests and older children. The recognition of these concerns led to the creation of service processes from a child's-eye view.

For instance, what can be more disappointing than standing in line at Big Thunder Mountain with your family but not being tall enough to enter the ride? And what do your parents do when their turn comes? Must they leave you alone, or stand in line twice so each can ride the roller coaster? Instead, there is a process designed to solve this common dilemma. One parent can stay with the child while the other takes the ride. At the conclusion of the ride, the waiting parent may board immediately. And what about the child who can't ride at all? Cast members have a supply of special certificates that entitle the child to board the ride without waiting in line whenever he or she is tall enough.

Often small children do not find much to interest them in Epcot's World Showcase, so for them there is Kidcot. Kidcot includes a craft or activity in each of the national pavilions designed especially for smaller children. Every child also gets a discovery booklet that they fill out as they move from country to country. Similarly, in Downtown Disney's Marketplace, the boredom almost every small child feels when shopping is alleviated with a set of stickers that children can collect into a book as they move from shop to shop.

Again, service-attention processes designed specifically for guests who don't fit the average profile contribute to a better experience for the guests with special needs and those in their parties.

Guests with Disabilities

Every organization serves customers with disabilities, and today, it is not only good business to provide for their special needs, it is also legally required. Several basic principles apply when designing service attention for guests with disabilities:

- Whenever possible, give guests with disabilities mainstream access to your organization. For example, at the Disney resorts and parks, every effort is made to provide access through the main entrance of attractions.

This way, guests can stay with their parties and enjoy the property along with everyone else.

- Since not all disabilities are obvious, find ways to allow guests to communicate their special needs without forcing them to explain them repeatedly. At Walt Disney World, for example, there are three different types of Special Assistance Passes that guests can carry to communicate their needs to cast members.

- Communicate the resources available to guests with disabilities at the widest possible level. All of our cast members are given basic training and guidance in assisting these guests in the Traditions program. In addition, Disney University offers specialized training to managers and key cast members who have high levels of guest contact.

- Finally, communicate available resources directly to your guests. For instance, Walt Disney World offers a special guidebook detailing the resources and one-to-one assistance available at Guest Services locations.

There are a host of resources available at Disney resorts and parks for guests with disabilities. Among them are audio tours for those with visual disabilities. There also are wireless audio boosters, sign-language performances, and reflective captioning for those with hearing disabilities. There are guest-assistance packages containing scripts, flashlights, and pen and paper offered at many of our shows and attractions. All of these are meant to ensure that disabled guests get the best show possible.

All organizations have customers with needs that fall outside their standard processes. When Disney Institute client East Jefferson General Hospital examined its patient base, it found that oncology patients had very different needs and desires from maternity patients. Oncology patients wanted quiet, private waiting areas where they could meet with their families while avoiding the general population and repeated explanations of their illnesses. Maternity patients, on the other hand, wanted to celebrate their new arrivals with friends and family. In response, East Jefferson created different processes and settings for each group of patients. The hospital provided peace, quiet, and privacy outside the mainstream for oncology patients and a festive atmosphere with extra space for visitors for the maternity patients.

Before we move on, take a few minutes to identify your customers who need service attention. How can you improve their service experience?

SERVICE PROCESS DEBUGGING

As mentioned earlier, Disney has a longstanding tradition of plussing to improve the products and services offered to guests. When plussing is applied to improving service processes, we call it debugging. Every service process needs to be debugged to work in the best interests of guests.

Debugging may seem at odds with the maxim of "do it right the first time," but the reality of business and life is that doing anything perfectly from the start is a relatively rare occurrence.

First, even though we strive to create flawless organizations, we are dealing with living systems, and they are never completely predictable. Second, even if we could perfect our organizations, that perfection is only achieved for a short time. New technologies and techniques soon appear that allow us to make them even better.

Just ask the world's leading dedicated toy and juvenile products retailer, Wayne, New Jersey–based Toys "R" Us. In 1948, founder Charles Lazarus reinvented the retail toy industry—and retailing in general—when he created the first self-serve toy supermarket, a one-stop shop for everything any kid could ever want. Today's big-box specialty retail chains owe their very existence to Mr. Lazarus's business model. Toys "R" Us is a $13.9-billion company with more than 1,600 stores and about 70,000 employees.

You might think that Toys "R" Us has its business down pat, but its management doesn't think that way. Times change and so do customers, and the company continues to reinvent itself and its business processes. Over the years, it expanded internationally, added a catalog sales business as the home shopping trend began to build, and with the advent of the Internet, the company started its drive to dominate toy sales in cyberspace.

The company also periodically redesigns its stores to improve the customer experience and enhance results. In 1999, for instance, the company's leaders understood that Charles Lazarus's super toy store was no longer as unique as it had been a decade earlier, so they decided to up the ante in the industry once again by adding practical magic to the sales mix. After benchmarking its Quality Service at Walt Disney World and training an implementation team at Disney Institute, Toys "R" Us introduced a new brand of service. On the evening of June 13, 1999, every associate and manager in North America, including two thousand national support staff associates, learned the basics of creating magical service experiences, delighting their guests, and a new service vision and vocabulary. At midnight on June 14, the "magic moment" struck, and every employee knew that making practical magic for their guests was Toys "R" Us's new business.

Like Toys "R" Us, you can recognize the realities of an ever-changing marketplace and continually improve your business model and processes or you can insist that you got it right the first time and stick your head in the sand. If you chose the first option, read on. If not, consider what Bob Iger recently told the *Financial Times* about Disney's studio entertainment business: "The business model that underpins the movie business is changing. If we don't adapt to the change there won't be a business—that's my exhortation to my team."[9] Indeed, the same eventually holds true for every business. Standing still is not a viable option.

Opportunities for the improvement of service processes tend to arise from two kinds of circumstances. The first kinds grow out of design flaws or oversights or the availability of improved technologies. We, as service organizations, own those problems. The second kinds emerge directly out of the needs of our guests, or guest-owned actions. Let's take a closer look at these two kinds of improvement opportunities.

Debugging Flawed Processes

One of the most popular features at the Disney theme parks is the ability to meet and be photographed with Mickey Mouse and the entire cast of Disney characters. Character appearances have been a standard part of the guest experience since 1955, when Disneyland first opened. For guests, however, spending the time they wanted with our characters has not always been a simple task.

When guestology studies at Walt Disney World revealed the desire for greater access to character appearances and the difficulty of navigating the crowds that quickly formed around the characters, the resorts and parks began to debug the experience. First came Toontown, which brought the characters into one area that could be managed for the best guest experience. Then fixed character greeting locations were established throughout the parks, and their locations were communicated in guidebooks and with signage. Finally, to ensure that our guests could find Pocahontas or Snow White or their favorite character, CHIP was created. CHIP is the Character Hotline and Information Program, a telephone number that every cast member can call to tell our guests exactly when and where to find each character.

Sometimes debugging a process flaw requires inconveniencing a guest, such as when a product must be recalled. Anyone who has witnessed the public-relations nightmares that ensue when these incidents are mishandled knows they can be very damaging to an organization's reputation and bottom line. On the other hand, a well-conducted debugging can enhance both customer loyalty and long-term profits.

The Volkswagen Group experienced the latter phenomenon soon after the launch of its popular New Beetle in 1998. The company had undertaken the most elaborate launch in its history to celebrate the rebirth of its classic VW Bug. To introduce the new car to its dealers, the company brought nine thousand employees and family members from its North American headquarters and its dealership network to Walt Disney World for seminars and some fun. The consumer launch was even more extensive, featuring marketing and advertising campaigns that blanketed North America.

After a hugely successful launch that had car buyers signing up on waiting lists for the New Beetle, the company discovered that a wiring assembly in some of the cars could have been installed in a way that might lead to chafing. The company was concerned that, in the worst case, this had the potential to cause a fire. In a textbook example of service debugging, the company authorized a full recall. No customer would ever have to wonder if his or her new car was safe. To compensate their customers for the inconvenience of having to return their new cars to the dealer for repair, Volkswagen authorized a $100 allowance per customer. To apologize, dealers were authorized to spend the money any way the customer wanted.

The company's fast, sensitive response saved the day. Not only did its customer satisfaction numbers remain constant, the company actually received thank-you letters from New Beetle owners. The car, which had been targeted to eventually build to annual sales of fifty thousand vehicles, sold over seventy thousand units in its first year.

Improving Outdated Processes

The ticketing system at the Disney parks is a good example of a debugging opportunity that arose from changes in technology. The ticketing process had grown extremely complicated over the decades. Cast members spent more time worrying about tickets than serving guests. At one time, there were two thousand active categories of paper tickets to manage, and ticket changes required at least a three-week lead time. On top of that, the printed tickets were useable prior to their issuance, so there were many loss-control and security issues inherent in the system.

The rapid development of automated networks and smart-card technology allowed Walt Disney World to completely reengineer the process. A new Automated Ticketing System (ATS) based on magnetically coded, credit card–size tickets was put into place. Soon, there were only eight categories of tickets, which could be encoded in an infinite number of variations, and tickets did not become "live" until the point of sale. Even better, the encoded card could be simply swiped at the automated turnstiles located at the entrance to the parks, leaving the cast plenty of time to greet and assist guests.

Disney's "Magic Your Way" tickets are another example of debugging designed to improve the guest experience. In this program, guests are given choices that allow them to purchase tickets to our theme parks that best fit their needs. They can purchase tickets based on the number of days they will be visiting and the number of parks they plan to visit each day and save on the price accordingly.

Debugging Guest-owned Processes

Guests sometimes make mistakes. If they are abandoned to deal with the results of those problems alone, we are abrogating our responsibility to create Quality Service experiences. Providing a magical guest experience means solving the problems our guests create with the same dedication we show in attacking problems we create ourselves. A perfect example of a successfully debugged guest-owned problem is the solution, described in Chapter 1, that Walt Disney World cast members found to help guests who had forgotten where they had parked their cars.

Sometimes the guest-owned problem is very minor indeed. A guest might have a squeaky wheel on a baby stroller or lose a button or, as anyone with poor vision well knows, lose one of those tiny, impossible-to-find screws that hold a pair of eyeglasses together. Enter the Magic Pouch. The security cast members at Epcot invented the Magic Pouch in response to the minor problems that guests commonly encounter. Each now wears a pouch containing the solutions to those common problems: a can of lubricating oil, a sewing kit and safety pins, and even an eyeglasses-repair kit. Voilá—problem solved, and guest experience enhanced.

Our exploration of the main points on the Quality Service Compass is almost complete. We've explored how to center our efforts on guests and discover what they want, how to create quality standards and a common purpose, and the three major service-delivery systems that all companies share: cast, setting, and process. There is, however, one compass point left, the most important of all: Integration—the job of putting everything together to create the practical magic of Quality Service.

Quality Service Cues

Take a process orientation to service delivery. Roughly three-quarters of service is delivered via processes. Processes are the policies, tasks, and procedures used to deliver service.

Collect and analyze combustion statements. Combustion statements indicate service issues that need to be solved. Listen to and study your guests to identify and optimize those issues before combustion points become explosion points.

Optimize guest flow throughout the service experience. Create the perfect service flow by optimizing the operation of products and services, allowing guests to self-manage their experience, and effectively managing unavoidable waits.

Equip your cast to communicate with guests. Fielding questions immediately is an important component of customer satisfaction. Provide your cast with the right information in the right manner at the right time.

Create processes for guests who need service attention. Treat all of your guests like VIPs—very important, very individual people. Identify guests who need service attention, such as children, international customers, and people with disabilities, then implement processes designed to ensure they get a positive service experience and communicate those processes throughout the organization.

Debug service processes continuously. "Plus" your service processes at every opportunity. Fix design flaws and oversights, adapt new technologies and techniques, and solve your customers' problems before they ask for help.

CHAPTER 6

The Magic of Integration

By the early 1940s, there was no disputing that The Walt Disney Company had become the world's leading animation studio. The staff, the facilities and equipment, and the filmmaking process had combined to create the greatest animated entertainment audiences had ever seen. Walt Disney had harnessed the magic of integration and, in doing so, turned out great films, such as the animation classic *Snow White*, which premiered on December 21, 1937, and quickly became the highest-grossing film of all time.

Whether by plan or intuition, Walt had built the capabilities of the three delivery systems that all organizations share. His *cast*, the studio staff, was the best in world. Thanks to extensive in-house training and apprenticeship programs, the company was continually building the competence and expertise of its workforce. Walt was also busy constructing a world-class *setting* for the production of animated films. In 1940, the company began moving into its brand-new studio in Burbank, which Walt had built with his usual attention to detail. Finally, step by step and innovation by innovation, Walt had created a *process* capable of producing a full-length animation feature.

When Walt brought these delivery systems together, his dream of turning animation into a respected form of entertainment was fully realized. "All the Hollywood brass turned out for my cartoon!" he remembered long after the triumphant opening of *Snow White*. "That was the thing. And it went way back to when I first came out here and I went to my first premiere. I'd never seen one in my life. I saw all these Hollywood celebrities comin' in and I just had a funny feeling. I just hoped that someday they'd be going to a premiere of a cartoon. Because people would depreciate the cartoon. You know, they'd kind of look down."[1]

Walt put the three delivery systems of Quality Service together once again to create the unique entertainment known as Disneyland. He staffed his new kind of amusement park with a new kind of employee. Hucksters and the sour-faced need not apply. Instead, Walt insisted on a clean-cut image and a permanent smile. And he established the first corporate university to teach his cast how to treat Disneyland's guests. The setting was planned, constructed, and plussed down to the smallest detail. The service processes, such as the timing of the Jungle Boat cruise, were refined and executed down to the second.

The result, not counting Black Sunday—that rough opening

day, when the crowds simply overran the new park—was a resounding success. Within seven weeks of its opening, one million guests had visited Disneyland. The attendance exceeded the company's targeted goals by 50 percent, and guests were spending 30 percent more than anticipated. In 1950, the Disney Company had revenues of $5 million. In 1955, when Disneyland opened, revenues were $27 million. And by year-end 1959, the company's revenues had grown to $70 million. The magic of integration had turned Walt Disney's cartoon studio into an entertainment empire.[2]

Integration is still working its magic throughout The Walt Disney Company today. Every moviegoer who sat entranced through the *Toy Story* films, the *Pirates of the Caribbean* films, *The Lion King*, and a slew of other Disney hits was treated to an integrated dose of Quality Service. Every one of the millions of annual visitors to the Disney resorts and parks around the world gets the same integrated guest experience, even though they would surely not describe their vacation in exactly those terms.

> *Get a good idea and stay with it. Dog it, and work at it until it's done and done right.*
> —Walt Disney

PUTTING QUALITY SERVICE TOGETHER

Here's one scene you will never witness: Your neighbors have just returned home after a visit to a Disney park; say it's Tokyo

Disneyland. "How did it go?" you ask. "Wow," say the parents, "you've gotta experience the common purpose at Tokyo Disneyland to believe it. Those folks know their quality standards."

"Yeah," chime in the kids, "that Fantasyland, boy, talk about a performance culture. And you have to see how they combine cast, setting, and process in Pooh's Hunny Hunt to deliver Quality Service!"

Disney's guests are surrounded by all of those things, but elements such as quality standards and delivery systems provide the infrastructure of Quality Service, and like many infrastructures, this one is supposed to be invisible to the customer. Like a surfer on the Internet who effortlessly jumps from site to site, navigating around the globe with a click of the mouse, guests can see and judge the service supported by the infrastructure—but they don't need to know how it is constructed.

When your neighbors rave about their experiences staying at a Disney resort or at an attraction in one of the parks, what they are really describing is how well all of the points on the Quality Service Compass have been integrated to deliver a seamless, magical guest experience. *Integration* is the operative word. It is the work of bringing all of the elements of Quality Service together to create a complete experience. It is the critical, final point on the Quality Service Compass. Integration enables us to achieve Quality Service by identifying which details to attend to and what guest expectations to exceed.

When the elements of a system are properly integrated, the result is a booster rocket for progress. The value of the entire organization becomes greater than the sum of its parts. This multiplier effect happens because the effective operation of one system not only achieves its own goals, it also supports and enhances the goals of other systems. For instance, the Whispering Canyon Café in Wilderness Lodge in Walt Disney World opens onto the main lobby, and its cast acts and is costumed like characters from the Old West. As a result, the cast does more than simply serve food and drink. They entertain the guests in the restaurant with their colorful actions and accents, and they add to the show in the entire main lobby. The cast is adding value to the setting.

But the elements of a system must be *properly* integrated. It is always possible to make one element more effective at the cost of another. Disneyland Paris could speed up the boat ride in the Pirates of Caribbean attraction and more guests would see the show each hour. The guest flow process would be more efficient, but what effect would that have on the cast, not to mention the ability of guests to enjoy the details of the setting? Elements in a system must be aligned to work together so they don't detract from each other.

Exactly what is integrated and aligned to create Quality Service? The simple answer is the quality standards of the organization and its primary delivery systems. The quality standards in the Disney parks—safety, courtesy, show, and efficiency—represent behaviors that fulfill our common goal, and the delivery systems—cast, setting, and process—are the distribution channels used to ensure that those standards reach guests. So the goal of integration is the delivery of your organization's quality standards to your customers via people, process, and place.

Every quality standard can be distributed over all three delivery systems. For example, at BoardWalk Resort at Walt Disney World, safety is delivered through the cast, setting, and processes. The cast is trained at the organizational and departmental levels in safety techniques. The setting delivers safety, too. One half of the boardwalk at the resort is supported by steel; it was designed as a fire lane and provides emergency access to the stores and restaurants lining the vintage Atlantic City oceanfront. Finally, safety is built into processes, such as the loading and unloading procedures on the water launches that bring guests to BoardWalk Resort from other parks and resorts. The standards of courtesy, show, and efficiency can also be distributed over all three delivery systems.

Even though all three delivery systems can distribute each quality standard, there are certain delivery systems that are especially well aligned with specific standards. At the Disney Institute, these are known as *headliners* because of the power inherent in these special combinations. For instance, although courtesy is delivered via setting and process, it is the cast that is especially suited to deliver the personal touch to guests. Likewise, the Disney standard of show is best communicated via setting, and efficiency is often a process-related issue. Headliners will vary depending on your organization's quality standards, but you should identify them and make sure that they receive special attention during the integration phase of Quality Service development.

Just because there are natural integration headliners doesn't mean the other two delivery systems can be ignored. The secondary systems are called *landmarks*, and they also offer fine opportunities to exceed guest expectations. It is important that a process delivers an efficient service experience, but many of us expect streamlined, time-saving transactions these days. When the cast and the layout of the organization streamline that experience even more, however, customers are often wowed.

THE INTEGRATION MATRIX

The Integration Matrix is a helpful tool that can guide you through the analysis and improvement of service. The matrix in the following diagram is a simple chart designed to track the distribution of quality standards through delivery systems. To build one of your own, create an expanded tic-tac-toe board with enough rows along the side to list your organization's quality standards and three columns across the top to accommodate the delivery systems of cast, setting, and process. Now insert your quality standards on the side, in priority order from top to bottom.

Take a moment to consider the boxes in the body of the matrix. Each represents an intersection between a single quality standard and a delivery system. In the upper-left-hand corner of the diagram, safety and cast are combined. In the lower-right-hand corner, efficiency and process meet. Each of these meetings represents a service moment of truth, a point

Integration Matrix

	Cast	Setting	Process
Safety			
Courtesy			
Show			
Efficiency			

at which you can affect the quality of the guest experience. In essence, each box asks a question of the creators of Quality Service. For example, in that upper-left-hand corner, the question is, how will your cast deliver safety to guests? In the lower right, how will your processes create a more efficient guest experience? By filling in the answers in each box, you can create a complete Quality Service experience.

The ability to design a fresh and fully integrated approach to the guest experience is just one of the uses of the Integration Matrix. It can also be used as a diagnostic tool to isolate, analyze, and brainstorm solutions to service lapses. You can fine-tune the matrix by imposing other parameters. For example, you could use it to identify effective *and* inexpensive approaches to creating service moments. Finally, the Integration Matrix is a useful benchmarking tool. It can be used to analyze a competitor's or a partner's service.

The level at which you can apply the matrix is similarly diverse. It can be used at the strategic level. For example, you might generate broad boundaries for Quality Service by using it to analyze and improve the end-to-end guest experience. You could also narrow the focus of the matrix to the departmental or single-process level by aiming it at sales, customer service, or collections. Or you can narrow the focus of the matrix even further by honing in on and expanding a single service moment—in essence concentrating on one box in the matrix. By adjusting the focus of the matrix, it becomes useful at all levels of the organization, from the senior leadership team to a group of frontline cast members who are charged with creating incremental improvements in their own show. Here is a look at a specific Integration Matrix drawn from the highly successful Star Guest Program implemented at Hong Kong Disneyland.

INTEGRATING THE STAR GUEST PROGRAM

The Star Guest Program was created in response to several challenges at Hong Kong Disneyland. The park was a huge hit from the day it opened, on September 12, 2005, but guestology revealed that something was not quite right. "In later months," explained Noble Coker, Vice President of Park Operations and Operations Development, "we noticed a trend of feedback from local guests expressing disappointment in some of our service offerings. Our cast found it difficult to stay motivated, and our leaders struggled to manage cast and guest expectations."[3]

When the park's leaders investigated the problem, they found that the Western version of Disney's Quality Service was not as well aligned with Chinese culture as it could have been. Many of our Chinese guests are more reserved than Westerners, and sometimes the friendliness of the cast makes them uncomfortable. In fact, guestology revealed that 90 percent of our local guests preferred to see someone else get personal recognition rather than themselves. Also, the Chinese tend not to verbally praise great service at the moment it is delivered; instead they will give a small gift at a later time. As a result, the cast found it difficult to stay motivated.

The Star Guest Program was conceived as a solution to these problems. It is a program that allows families or groups visiting Hong Kong Disneyland to pick up a Star Recognition Pack at City Hall on Main Street, U.S.A., and designate one of their party as a VIP guest. Star Guests wear a badge and receive special attention and experiences—Magical Moments that are created by the cast—during his or her visit, such as exclusive Meet & Greets and rides with characters and the chance to conduct the Disneyland band. The Star Guest also receives two recognition cards, which can be given to cast members who deliver superlative service.

There are many benefits to the program. It enables guests themselves to choose who will receive the cast's attention, eliminating potential discomfort. It involves the cast in creating and delivering Magical Moments—honing their Quality Service expertise. It provides guests with a culturally acceptable way to provide recognition and simultaneously builds cast morale. There is also one more valuable benefit: Hong Kong Disneyland first launched the Star Guest Program from March to May of 2009. Not only were these the slowest months in terms of annual attendance at the park, but it was also in the middle of the global financial crisis. So the publicity and guest interest in the program helped stimulate attendance.

In fact, all of these benefits were achieved in 2009. The cast created and delivered 185 different kinds of Magical Moments, becoming better Quality Service experts in the process. The Star Guest Program helped increase guest satisfaction: guest scores for "having a carefree visit" rose 19 percent, "friendliness of cast" gained 11 percent, and "overall experience" rose 10 percent. Guests gave the cast over 43,000 recognition cards; 928 of the cast members received special costume-approved recognition pins for receiving fifteen or more cards. And not least of all, the program drove a 10 percent rise in attendance in the midst of a global recession.

Of course, the Star Guest Program was developed using the same quality standards and delivery systems in use through Disney's parks and resorts business. Here's how the Integration Matrix can be used to analyze it.

The first questions, of course, involve the top service priority, the nonnegotiable quality standard of safety. How did the Star Guest Program ensure guest and cast safety? Happily, the answers to those questions were already well established at

Hong Kong Disneyland. The cast delivers a safe experience by being prepared for emergencies. They get the same property-wide and location-specific training that all Disney parks cast members receive. The physical setting and objects associated with the program were also vetted for safety. And the processes involved in delivering Magical Moments were evaluated first and foremost from a safety perspective.

	Cast	Setting	Process
Safety	Training in property-wide and local line-of-business safety techniques and policy	Ensure all objects and physical surroundings are safe for cast and guests; utilize existing safety elements in park	Evaluate and ensure safety as the first filter for all Magical Moments

By simply moving down to the next row on the Integration Matrix, we receive our next series of questions. This time, they cover the delivery of the standard of courtesy in the Star Guest Program preview experience. Since the delivery system of cast is the headliner for courtesy, Hong Kong Disneyland ensured that the cast played a primary role in delivering a courteous guest experience. For example, the park modified Disney's aggressive friendliness for the Chinese culture by focusing on the cultural mores and behaviors of its local guests. And extensive field coaching for cast and leaders was provided to ensure that their behaviors were sensitive to the local culture.

With actions of the headliner established, we can start thinking about how the landmark delivery systems extend the standard of courtesy. In the Star Guest Program, care and courtesy were built into the program by, for example, providing guests with recognition cards to give to cast members. The Star Guest process was also designed to ensure courteous treatment. For example, guests pick VIPs among themselves to eliminate the possibility of unwanted attention.

	Cast	Setting	Process
Courtesy	Modify behaviors for local culture; provide field coaching for cast and leaders	Provide recognition cards to guests to give to cast members	Create process in which guests pick VIPs themselves

Moving down to the third row in the Integration Matrix, we are confronted with a third set of questions. This time, we consider the quality standard of show and how it is delivered by the cast, setting, and process in the Star Guest Program. Starting with the headliner—in this case, setting—Hong Kong Disneyland designed and printed Star Recognition Packs for the guests, utilized the existing settings of the parks, and installed recognition boards and created a costume pin for the cast.

In this case the cast actually created the show, developing the 185 Magical Moments on their own. Then processes were developed to standardize and scale up the delivery of each of the Magical Moments, such as weekly prize drawings to motivate cast members and a leadership modeling process for demonstrating desired program behaviors.

	Cast	Setting	Process
Show	Cast creates Magical Moments themselves	Create Star Recognition Pack; install recognition boards for cast; create a Star Guest costume pin for high-performing cast members	Magical Moments processes created; biweekly prize drawings for cast; modeling process executed by leader

The final row in our analysis of the Star Guest Program asks questions about the quality standard of efficiency. The headliner here is the delivery system of process. Hong Kong Disneyland pursued efficiency via process in a variety ways. For example, metrics were identified, and usage of the Star Guest Program was thoroughly analyzed, with the results used to improve the program and individual Magical Moments. The costs of the Moments were studied, and when it was discovered that no-cost and low-cost Moments that had more personal interaction with cast members were often valued more highly by many guests, the focus was shifted to them. As an additional benefit of this measurement and analysis, paid Magical Moments, which created a new revenue stream, were introduced for those guests who expressed a desire for more elaborate experiences.

In what should start feeling like a familiar pattern, Hong Kong Disneyland then considered the landmark systems of cast and setting and how they could deliver an efficient Star Guest experience. For cast, the park conducted a trial run one week before the formal launch of the program to build confidence and surface any last-minute problems. It also formed a cross-functional leadership team to smooth implementation of Magical Moments that involved more than one line of business and functional area. In the setting box, the number of Star Recognition Packs was purposely limited so that cast members would not be overwhelmed by the need to deliver too many Magical Moments and to preserve the exclusivity of being a Star Guest for customers.

	Cast	Setting	Process
Efficiency	Conduct trial run for the cast; create cross-functional leadership team to smooth implementation of Magical Moments	Limit number of VIP guests by limiting number of Star Recognition Packs	Measure results of program and use to plus; focus on low- and no-cost Magical Moments; create additional revenue with upgrade option

This completes the Integration Matrix for the Star Guest Program, but there are a couple of ancillary points worth noting before we put it all together. First, to keep this case study manageable, we described only a few of the ideas used by Hong Kong Disneyland in each service box in the matrix. In fact, each box in the Star Guest Program has a long list of actions designed to deliver a magical service experience. Second, for clarity, we described the use of the matrix in a linear fashion. In reality, you can start anywhere and proceed as convenient. The important thing is that in the end every box has been thoroughly considered. With that in mind, here's what the Star Guest Program's completed Integration Matrix looks like:

The Star Guest Program Integration Matrix

	Cast	Setting	Process
Safety	Training in property-wide and local line-of-business safety techniques and policy	Ensure all objects and physical surroundings are safe for cast and guests; utilize existing safety elements in park	Evaluate and ensure safety as the first filter for all Magical Moments
Courtesy	Modify behaviors for local culture; provide field coaching for cast and leaders	Provide recognition cards to guests to give to cast members	Create process in which guests pick VIPs themselves
Show	Cast creates Magical Moments themselves	Create Star Recognition Pack; install recognition boards for cast; create a Star Guest costume pin for high-performing cast members	Magical Moments processes created; biweekly prize drawings for cast; modeling process executed by leader
Efficiency	Conduct trial run for the cast; create cross-functional leadership team to smooth implementation of Magical Moments	Limit number of VIP guests by limiting number of Star Recognition Packs	Measure results of program and use to plus; focus on low- and no-cost Magical Moments; create additional revenue with upgrade option

THREE ELEMENTS OF MAGICAL SERVICE MOMENTS

Bill Martin, one of the original Imagineers who helped design Disneyland, made the following observation about his experiences working with Walt Disney. "Walt used to say, 'I don't care what you can't do. I want to hear what you *can* do.' If there were fifteen ways to solve a problem, Walt was looking for all fifteen."[4] That is one reason why Walt would have liked the Integration Matrix.

One of the best features of the Integration Matrix is that it leaves room for more than one right answer when creating a great service moment. As you begin to use the Integration Matrix to develop the features of service experiences, each intersection of quality standard and delivery system will yield numerous alternatives. You may choose to implement one idea or all of them or any number in between.

When the time comes to analyze all of the ideas you have generated to populate the Integration Matrix and decide which ideas to implement, there are three features of great service moments to keep in mind. They are high-touch, high-show, and high-tech.

High-touch refers to the need to build guest interaction into the service experience. For the most part, we humans enjoy connecting with each other. So if we create service moments that give guests a chance to participate, make choices, and interact with the cast, they will connect more intimately with the experience and the organization that is providing it. High-touch is a quality that cast is particularly adept at providing.

At the Disney parks and resorts, when you see a cast member taking a family picture for a guest, you are witnessing a service that offers high-touch. When you call the WDW-Dine Line at Walt Disney World to make a priority seating at a restaurant, you are seeing high-touch applied to a process. And when you stand in front of one of the twenty-two pieces of Enchanted Art hanging aboard the *Disney Dream* and it senses you are there and springs into motion, you are getting high-touch from a setting.

High-show refers to the need to build vivid presentations into the guest experience. When we choose service solutions that are high-show, guests enjoy colorful, memorable experiences—the kind that they will talk about to others for months and perhaps years to come. High-show is a quality that is closely aligned to the delivery system of setting, so be sure to think about how to build it into designs for your organization's physical assets.

Disney's Grand Floridian Resort & Spa is a good example of a high-show setting. Patterned after the grand hotels of the late 1800s, it is a nine-hundred-room trip back to the Victorian Era, and every detail supports the show. You can see high-show in Epcot's IllumiNations program. Every night, fireworks, lasers, fountains, and music are combined to create a spectacular wrap-up to a day at the park. And visit Disney's Hollywood Studios for a look at how cast can deliver high-show. There, the Streetmosphere performers are costumed and perform as the characters you would likely encounter in the streets of mythic Hollywood. Starlets, taxi drivers, and even autograph hounds entertain guests as they move through the park.

High-tech refers to the need to build speed, accuracy, and expertise into service solutions. When we do a good job of creating high-tech service, we give guests the gift of time, build products and services that approach the cutting edge of the possible, and, often, maximize our own profits. Processes are particularly well suited to deliver high-tech, so as you create and improve processes, think about how they can be made more efficient and entertaining with technology.

The automated ticketing systems at the Disney parks support a process that encompasses the feature of high-tech. To see high-tech in a setting, take a spin on the Rock 'n' Roller Coaster. The vehicles accelerate from zero to sixty miles per hour in 2.8 seconds, exert five g-forces of pressure on the rider, and with five speakers per seat, it sounds as if the rock band came along for the ride.

Finally, to see high-tech at work in the delivery system of cast, take a behind-the-scenes look at the paramedics and firefighters at the Reedy Creek Emergency Services. They employ many high-tech solutions to protect the cast members and guests of Walt Disney World. To get a feel for what that means, consider that since the property opened in 1971, there has been less than $200,000 in structural fire loss. A single house fire can easily exceed that figure.

High-touch, high-show, and high-tech. As you explore the ways to make the most of your service moments, be sure to keep all three features in mind.

ONE FINAL TOOL—THE STORYBOARD

There is one more effective technique for the Quality Service toolkit—storyboarding. Storyboards are a great way to map out a service solution and to build a plan for its implementation. The technique is used throughout The Walt Disney Company as well as throughout the motion picture industry. But what many of those who use it don't know is that it originated in the Disney animation studios back in the 1930s.

According to Walt, the storyboard was invented by Webb Smith, an animator and one of the first storymen at the studio. When Webb planned a story, he would draw it instead of describing the action in words. At first, he simply spread the drawings out over the floor of his office, but soon he graduated to pinning them in order onto the walls. In this way, the unfolding story gained a valuable visual dimension. According to legend, Walt was none too happy with the innovation. He had just redecorated the offices, and the marred walls in Webb's office stuck out like a sore thumb. But Walt also recognized the order imposed by the posted drawings and the ease with which the entire feature could be analyzed and manipulated. So he ordered four- by eight-foot corkboards, and the storyboard was born.[5]

Soon every Disney cartoon first saw life on a storyboard, and the boards themselves moved to new departments as the project progressed. The storymen would pitch their ideas to Walt on a storyboard; color and sound were both added using the storyboard as reference point. When Walt hijacked the studio's animators to design the attractions for Disneyland, they brought the storyboard along with them. And today, it has evolved into a ubiquitous technique among the Imagineers. Here's how they describe its use:

THE MAGIC OF INTEGRATION

The first step in developing a three-dimensional world is to see it in two-dimensional storyboards. . . . For each ride, show, or attraction, a logical story sequence is created. Almost every aspect of the project is broken down into progressive scene sketches, called storyboard panels, that reflect the beginning, middle, and end of our guest's park experience.

The boards are eventually covered with every written thought, idea, and rough sketch we can come up with. If need be, a separate set of storyboards is developed for the sole purpose of establishing the camera shots required for the videos or film that may be part of the attraction. As they are fine-tuned, the boards are used as a presentation tool to sell the idea to management and to explain the concept to all of the Imagineering departments that will contribute to the evolution of the project.

A completed storyboard offers us the first chance to experience a new ride or show and see how the idea might— or might not—work.[6]

As might already be obvious, the storyboard is also an effective way to visualize and organize the development of the service solutions generated by the Integration Matrix. It offers a way to map the experience from a guest's perspective and improve and troubleshoot the proposed action before it ever gets off the, well, storyboard.

Here are two fast guidelines for storyboarding:

- For the nonartists among us, don't be intimidated by the use of drawings. At Disney, we have plenty of great

183

artists, but storyboarding is not about the beauty of the drawings. It is about the ability to see and consider ideas through your guests' eyes.

- Don't restrict the storyboard to drawings. Pin up fabric swatches, color samples, photos, text, brainstorming ideas, and anything else that helps communicate a better image of the intended project. Any one of these items might trigger a breakthrough that will take the level of your service another notch higher.

So this is how Quality Service comes together at The Walt Disney Company. A common purpose generates quality standards. The standards are defined and delivered using three basic systems that every organization shares: its people, its physical assets, and its processes. Finally, all three are integrated and aligned. That is the business behind the Disney brand of magic.

You have completed a full revolution around the Quality Service Compass. We've pulled back the curtain and shown you how the level of Quality Service that has made our company a world-class benchmark is created. And with the generous permission and assistance of a select group of Disney Institute clients, you have seen how organizations in business, education, health care, and government have applied the elements of the Quality Service Compass to improve their own guests' experiences.

Now it's time to put it to work in your organization and create some practical magic of your own.

Quality Service Cues

Build a service organization greater than the sum of its parts with integration. Integration is the work of aligning and distributing your service standards over the three delivery systems of cast, setting, and process.

Meet guest expectations with headliners; then plus the experience to exceed expectations. Headliners are those combinations of standards and delivery systems that are natural matches. At the Disney parks and resorts, they are cast and courtesy, setting and show, and process and efficiency. The remaining combinations can be used to distribute service standards in unexpected ways to surprise and delight guests.

Make the Integration Matrix part of your organizational toolbox. The Integration Matrix is an expanded tic-tac-toe board that combines service standards and delivery systems. Use it to analyze and manage the design and development of Quality Service.

Manage every service moment. On the Integration Matrix, each combination of a service standard and a delivery system represents a service moment of truth. Each should be fully considered and developed to deliver a magical service moment.

Choose service solutions that are high-touch, high-show, and high-tech. When analyzing service solutions, look for those that meet a guest's need for interaction, vivid presentation, and efficiency.

Plan and manage solution implementations using storyboards. Use storyboards—visual maps of service solutions—as an aid to implementation.

About the Authors

Disney Institute is the global professional-training arm of The Walt Disney Company. One of the most recognized names in professional development, Disney Institute travels the world offering engaging seminars, workshops, and presentations as well as fully customized programming. Immersive learning experiences are also offered at Disney destinations in the United States, Europe, and Asia, enabling participants to go behind the scenes and see firsthand how business theory drives operational excellence. The Disney Institute client roster includes Fortune 500 companies as well as a wide range of small businesses, non-profits, and government agencies. To learn more, please visit www.disneyinstitute.com, www.facebook.com/disneyinstitute, www.twitter.com/disneyinstitute, or call 321-939-4600.

Theodore Kinni (tedkinni@cox.net) is an award-winning business writer and senior editor for *strategy+business* magazine. He has authored and collaborated on fourteen business books. Ted is a member of the National Book Critics Circle and the Society of American Business Editors and Writers. He lives in Williamsburg, Virginia, with his wife and writing partner, Donna.

End Notes

Chapter 1

1. Kelvin Bailey's recollections of his trip with Walt Disney are recorded in *Remembering Walt: Favorite Memories of Walt Disney* by Amy Boothe Green and Howard Green (Disney Editions, 1999), pp. 178–179.
2. See Bob Iger's Letter to Shareholders in The Walt Disney Company's 2010 annual report (http://a.media.global. go.com/corporate/investors/annual_report/2010/media/ global/pdf/letter-to-shareholders.pdf).
3. The quote appears in the Participant's Manual for the Disney Institute's Disney Approach to Quality Service for Healthcare Professionals seminar.
4. See Suzy Wetlaufer's interview with Michael Eisner, "Commonsense and Conflict," in the Jan–Feb 2000 issue of *Harvard Business Review*.
5. See *The Experience Economy* by B. Joseph Pine II and James H. Gilmore (Harvard Business School Press, 1999), pp. 11–12.
6. The quote appears in *Walt Disney: Famous Quotes* (Disney Kingdom Editions, 1994), p. 36.

7. See "Secrets to success at the 'happiest place on earth,'" *Phoenix Focus*, November 2010 (http://www.phoenix.edu/ alumni/phoenix-focus/2010/11/secrets-to-success-at-the- happiest-place-on-earth.html).
8. John Hench's quote appears in *Remembering Walt: Favorite Memories of Walt Disney* by Amy Boothe Green and Howard Green (Disney Editions, 1999), p. 156.

Chapter 2

1. For more detail on the role of audience see Bob Thomas's *Walt Disney: An American Original* (Hyperion, 1994).
2. The quote appears in *Walt Disney: Famous Quotes* (Disney Kingdom Editions, 1994), p. 9.
3. Kurt Russell's quote appears in *Remembering Walt: Favorite Memories of Walt Disney* (Disney Editions, 1999), p. 45.
4. Tony Baxter relates this story in his interview with Didier Ghez in issue no. 22 of *"E" Ticket Magazine*.
5. See Bob Thomas's *Walt Disney: An American Original*, p. 263.
6. See *Remembering Walt: Favorite Memories of Walt Disney* (Disney Editions, 1999), p. 166.
7. See *Walt Disney: Famous Quotes* (Disney Kingdom Editions, 1994), p. 21.
8. The statistic and quote appear in James Collins and Jerry Porras's article "Building Your Company's Vision" in *Harvard Business Review*, September–October 1996.
9. The italics are Thomas Peters and Robert Waterman's. The quote appears on p. 168 of *In Search of Excellence: Lessons from America's Best-Run Companies* (Warner Books, 1984).

10. Woods's quote appears in "Great Expectations," in Government Executive, March 1, 2000 (http://www.govexec.com/gpp/0300osfa.htm).
11. Collins and Porras, "Building Your Company's Vision."
12. Bruce Johnson's quote appears on p. 113 of *Walt Disney Imagineering: A Behind the Dreams Look at Making the Magic Real* (Hyperion, 1996).
13. Marty Sklar's memory appears in Beth Dunlop's *Building a Dream: The Art of Disney Architecture* (Abrams, 1996), p. 14.

Chapter 3

1. See Robert Lacey's *Ford: The Men and the Machine* (Little, Brown, 1986) for a history of the Ford family and company. Henry Ford's quote appears on p. 305.
2. The quote appears in Richard Schickel's *The Disney Version* (Ivan R. Dee, 1997), p. 178.
3. See Bob Thomas's *Walt Disney* (Hyperion, 1994) for more detail on the development of the Disney Art School. The quote appears on p. 124.
4. Ibid., p. 143.
5. *Walt Disney: Famous Quotes* (Disney Kingdom Editions, 1994), p. 80.
6. The quote appears in the transcript of Tom Staggs's presentation at a Feb. 17, 2011, Disney Investor Conference (http://corporate.disney.go.com/news/parks_resorts/WDPR%20-%20Tom%20Staggs%20-%20Investor%20Conference.pdf).
7. *Training*, October 1999, p. 58.

8. For a more detailed description and photographs of the Casting Center, see Beth Dunlop's *Building a Dream: The Art of Disney Architecture* (Abrams, 1996). The quotes from Robert Stern, Beth Dunlop, and Tim Johnson appear on pp. 77–80.
9. Richard Parks's quote appears in Leon Rubis's article "Disney Show & Tell," in the April 1998 issue of *HR Magazine*.
10. Start was acquired by Holland's USG People, which in 2006 ranks fourth in Europe in the field of staffing, secondment, and HR services.

Chapter 4

1. The phrase appears on p. 134 of Bob Thomas's *Walt Disney: An American Original* (Hyperion, 1994).
2. The quote appears on p. 200 of Richard Schickel's *The Disney Version* (Ivan R. Dee, 1997).
3. For more on *Fantasia* and all of the Disney animated films, see Bob Thomas's *Disney's Art of Animation: From Mickey Mouse to Hercules* (Hyperion, 1997).
4. Walt's quote appears in Dave Smith's *The Quotable Walt Disney* (Disney Editions, 2001), p. 57
5. Tony Baxter quote appears on p. 14 of Beth Dunlop's *Building a Dream* (Abrams, 1996).
6. Ibid., p. 16.
7. The quote appears on p. 221 of Michael Eisner's *Work In Progress: Risking Failure, Surviving Success* (Hyperion, 1999).

END NOTES

8. The quote appears in "The Disney Approach to Quality Service for Healthcare Professionals, Participant's Manual."

9. Walt Disney's quote appears on p. 90 of *Walt Disney Imagineering* (Hyperion, 1996).

10. John Hench's quote appeared without attribution in "The First Twenty Years: From Disneyland to Walt Disney World, A Pocket History," which was distributed to cast members in 1976.

11. Walt Disney's quote appears on p. 9 of *Walt Disney Imagineering* (Hyperion, 1996).

12. See Birnbaum's *Walt Disney World 2000: the Official Guide* (Hyperion, 1999) for descriptions of the Disney attractions. The Haunted Mansion is featured on p. 102.

13. Kevin Post is quoted in "The Price of Admission," *Human Resource Executive*, June 16, 2000.

14. The quote appears on p. 13 of Bob Thomas's *Walt Disney: An American Original* (Hyperion, 1994).

15. The quote appears on p. 90 of *Walt Disney Imagineering* (Hyperion, 1996).

16. Ibid., p. 95.

17. Ibid., p. 130.

18. See *Walt Disney: Famous Quotes* (Disney Kingdom Editions, 1994), p. 29.

19. See Scott Kirsner's "Hack the Magic" in the March 1998 issue of *Wired* magazine for a good look at the technological systems used to run Walt Disney World and for the quote.

20. See "Disney spreads a little magic to water kingdom" by Zuleika Sedgley, *South China Morning Post*, April 25, 2011.

Chapter 5

1. See Bob Thomas's *Walt Disney: An American Original* (Hyperion, 1994) for a full account of the early years.
2. The quote appears on p. 185 of *The Illusion of Life: Disney Animation* by Frank Thomas and Ollie Johnston (Hyperion, 1995). The book contains a detailed examination of the Disney animation process by two men who experienced it firsthand.
3. The quote appears on p. 102 of Richard Schickel's *The Disney Version* (Ivan R. Dee, 1997).
4. Walt Disney's quote appears on p. 244 of Bob Thomas's *Walt Disney* (Hyperion, 1994).
5. Ibid., p. 290.
6. See pp. 240–248 in Michael Eisner's *Work In Progress* (Hyperion, 1999) for a fuller description of the founding of the Disney Store retail chain. The quote appears on p. 244.
7. See pp. 272–273 of Bob Thomas's *Walt Disney* (Hyperion, 1994) for a fuller description of Disneyland's opening day.
8. See Jason Garcia's "New line for Haunted Mansion ride is a window to Disney's future," *Orlando Sentinel*, March 26, 2011 (http://articles.orlandosentinel.com/2011-03-26/entertainment/os-disney-haunted-mansion-lines-20110326_1_oldest-rides-soarin-chairman-john-pepper).

9. See Matthew Garrahan's article "Disney chief tells Hollywood it must rewrite the script to survive" in the October 26, 2009, issue of *Financial Times* (http://www.ft.com/cms/s/0/3ccbfc62-c1ce-11de-b86b-00144feab49a.html#ixzz1KSrWlFZ2).

Chapter 6

1. Walt Disney's quote appears in Bob Thomas's *Walt Disney: An American Original* (Hyperion, 1994), p. 141.
2. Ibid., p. 285.
3. See Noble Coker's "Service Excellence: See it in a cultural context" in *Leadership Excellence*, December 2009.
4. Bill Martin's quote appears on p. 102 of Amy Boothe Green and Howard Green's *Remembering Walt: Favorite Memories of Walt Disney* (Disney Editions, 1999).
5. The genesis of storyboarding is related on pps. 147–148 of Richard Schickel's *The Disney Version* (Ivan R. Dee, 1997).
6. The quoted material appears on p. 40 of *Walt Disney Imagineering* (Hyperion, 1996). Read the book for an in-depth look at the design-and-build process used by the Disney Imagineers.

Index

INDEX

INDEX

F

Fantasia (film), 88–89
Fantasound, 89
FASTPASS Service, 139
Films, animated, 2, 15, 27–28, 87–89
Finesilver, Jeff, 109
Ford, Henry, 57
France, Van, 47
Fuller, R. Buckminster, 94

G

Gelgota, Bill, 117
Georganna, Lori, 138
Gilmore, James, 10, 11
"Good Show/Bad Show," 71–72
Graham, Don, 58, 59
Grand Floridian Hotel & Spa, 4, 92, 180
Graves, Michael, 91, 92
Guestology, 18, 19–20
 compass, 36, 55
 components of, 32–35
 as context for service
  strategies, 19–20
 continued importance of, 31
 focus groups, 33, 55
 listening posts and, 32, 55
 mystery shoppers, 32
 surveys, 32, 34, 55
 techniques of, 32–35, 55

use of information developed
 by, 33, 34
utilization studies, 32, 55
Guest(s)
 barriers to satisfaction, 80
 changing expectations of, 34
 customizing service for, 74
 demographics, 34, 35–36
 desire for greater access to
  Disney characters, 156
 disabled, 151–153
 emotions, 38, 40–41
 exceeding expectations of,
  13–14, 17
 flow, 25, 134
 guiding experiences for,
  106–110
 interaction with, 74
 international, 149–150
 as judges of product, 28
 needs of, 14, 19, 36, 37, 40–41
 perceptions of wait time,
  134–142
 profiles of, 55
 psychographics, 36–39
 return rate, 17
 self-management of
  movement by, 136–137
 service guidelines, 73
 solving problems of, 25
 stereotypes, 38, 40–41

INDEX

INDEX